On Core Mathematics

Grade 1

HOUGHTON MIFFLIN HARCOURT

D0470251

Cover photo credit: Stock48/Corbis

Printed in the U.S.A.

ISBN 978-0-547-57522-3

17 18 19 20 0982 20 19 18 17 16

4500596297   ^B C D E F G

Table of Contents

Operations and Algebraic Thinking

▶ **Add and subtract within 20.**

▶ **Work with addition and subtraction equations.**

Number and Operations in Base Ten

▶ **Extend the counting sequence.**

▶ **Understand place value.**

▶ **Use place value understanding and properties of operations to add and subtract.**

Measurement and Data

Geometry

▶ **Reason with shapes and their attributes.**

© Houghton Mifflin Harcourt Publishing Company

Algebra • Use Pictures to Add To

3 cows   and   2 more cows   __5__ cows.

Draw circles around the animals added to the group. Write how many.

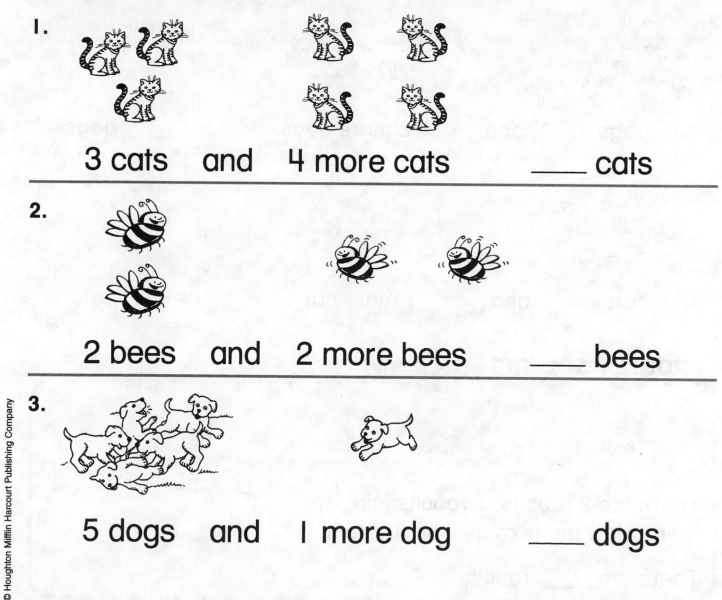

1.

3 cats   and   4 more cats   ____ cats

2.

2 bees   and   2 more bees   ____ bees

3.

5 dogs   and   1 more dog   ____ dogs

Operations and Algebraic Thinking

Algebra • Use Pictures to Add To

Write how many.

1.

5 horses   and   3 more horses   ____ horses

2.

3 dogs   and   2 more dogs   ____ dogs

3.

4 cats   and   1 more cat   ____ cats

PROBLEM SOLVING REAL WORLD

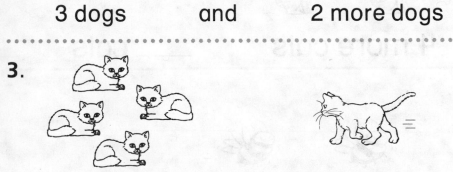

There are 2 rabbits. 5 rabbits join them. How many rabbits are there now?

There are ____ rabbits

Model Adding To

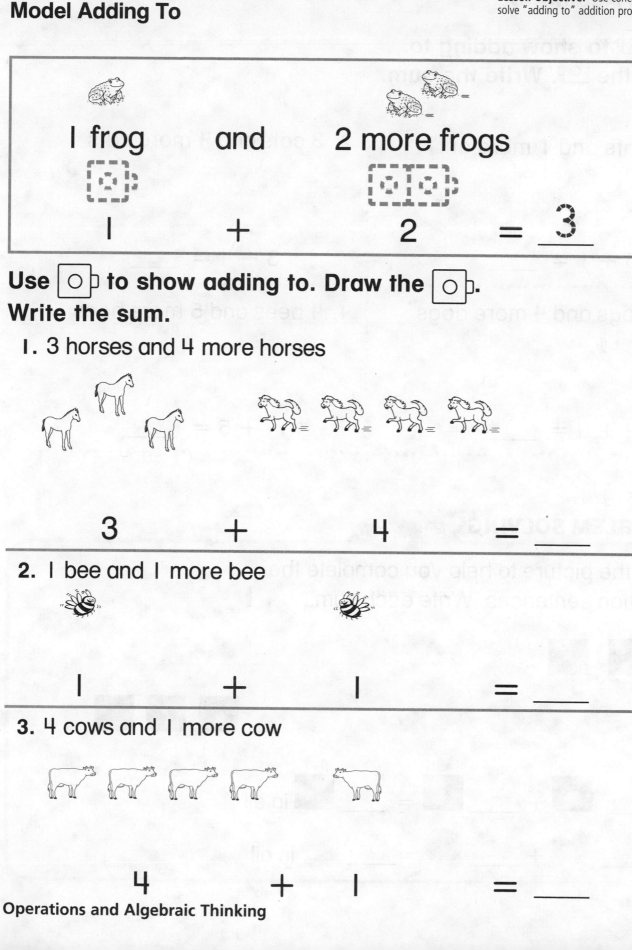

1 frog   and   2 more frogs

1 + 2 = 3

Use ◯ to show adding to. Draw the ◯.
Write the sum.

1. 3 horses and 4 more horses

3 + 4 = ___

2. 1 bee and 1 more bee

1 + 1 = ___

3. 4 cows and 1 more cow

4 + 1 = ___

Model Adding To

Use 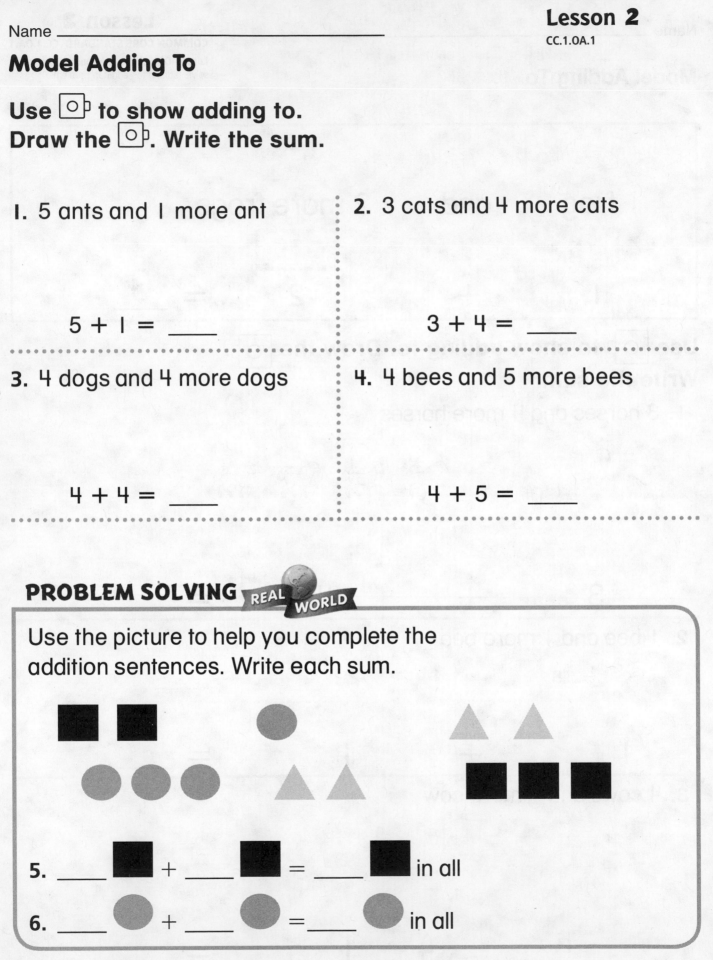 to show adding to.
Draw the ⌑. Write the sum.

1. 5 ants and 1 more ant

$$5 + 1 = \_\_\_$$

2. 3 cats and 4 more cats

$$3 + 4 = \_\_\_$$

3. 4 dogs and 4 more dogs

$$4 + 4 = \_\_\_$$

4. 4 bees and 5 more bees

$$4 + 5 = \_\_\_$$

PROBLEM SOLVING REAL WORLD

Use the picture to help you complete the addition sentences. Write each sum.

5. ___ ■ + ___ ■ = ___ ■ in all

6. ___ ● + ___ ● = ___ ● in all

4

Model Putting Together

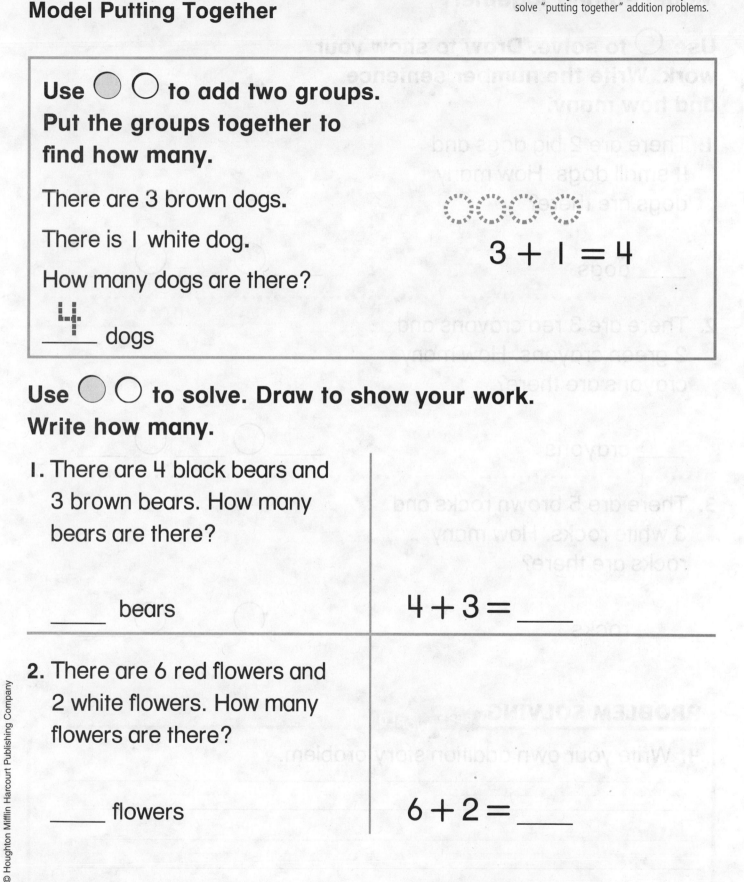

Use ◔ ◯ to add two groups.
Put the groups together to
find how many.

There are 3 brown dogs.

There is 1 white dog.

How many dogs are there?

__4__ dogs

$3 + 1 = 4$

Use ◔ ◯ to solve. Draw to show your work.
Write how many.

1. There are 4 black bears and
   3 brown bears. How many
   bears are there?

   _____ bears

   $4 + 3 =$ _____

2. There are 6 red flowers and
   2 white flowers. How many
   flowers are there?

   _____ flowers

   $6 + 2 =$ _____

Operations and Algebraic Thinking

Model Putting Together

Use ○ to solve. Draw to show your work. Write the number sentence and how many.

1. There are 2 big dogs and 4 small dogs. How many dogs are there?

   ____ dogs

   ___○___○___

2. There are 3 red crayons and 2 green crayons. How many crayons are there?

   ____ crayons

   ___○___○___

3. There are 5 brown rocks and 3 white rocks. How many rocks are there?

   ____ rocks

   ___○___○___

PROBLEM SOLVING REAL WORLD

4. Write your own addition story problem.

   _____
   _____
   _____
   _____

COMMON CORE STANDARD CC.1.OA.1
Lesson Objective: Solve adding to and putting together situations using the strategy *make a model*.

Problem Solving • Model Addition

Rico has 3 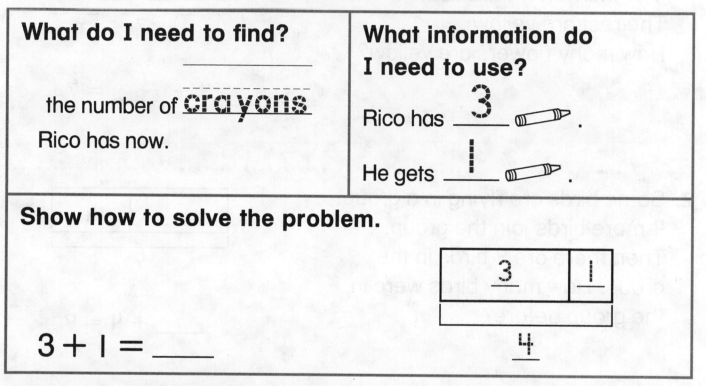. Then he gets 1 more 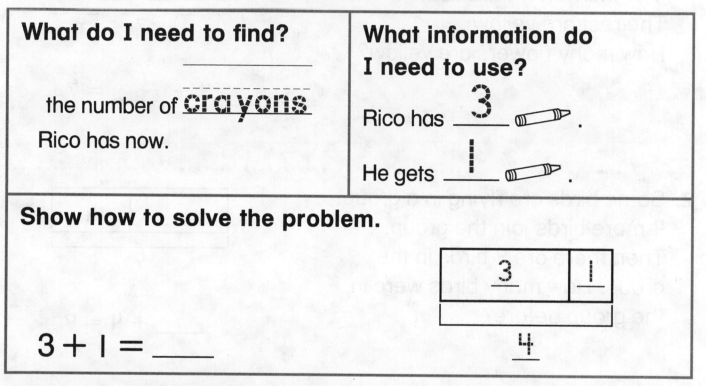.
How many 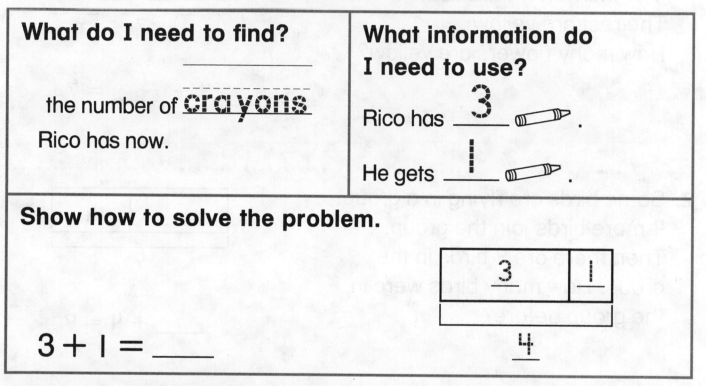 does he have now?

Unlock the Problem

What do I need to find?	**What information do I need to use?**
_____ the number of **crayons** Rico has now.	Rico has ____ **3** ____ . He gets ____ **1** ____ .

Show how to solve the problem.

3	1

4

$3 + 1 = $ ____

Read the problem. Use the bar model to solve.
Complete the model and the number sentence.

1. There are 5 birds flying.
   Then 3 more birds join them.
   How many birds are flying now?

5	3

____

$5 + 3 = $ ____

Problem Solving • Model Addition

Read the problem. Use the bar model to solve. Complete the model and the number sentence.

1. Dylan has 7 flowers.
   4 of the flowers are red.
   The rest are yellow.
   How many flowers are yellow?

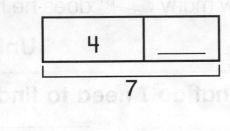

$$4 + \underline{\quad} = 7$$

2. Some birds are flying in a group.
   4 more birds join the group.
   Then there are 9 birds in the
   group. How many birds were in
   the group before?

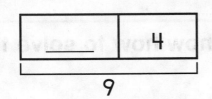

$$\underline{\quad} + 4 = 9$$

3. 6 cats are walking.
   1 more cat walks with them.
   How many cats are walking now?

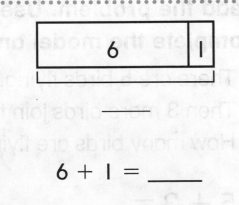

$$6 + 1 = \underline{\quad}$$

Algebra • Put Together Numbers to 10

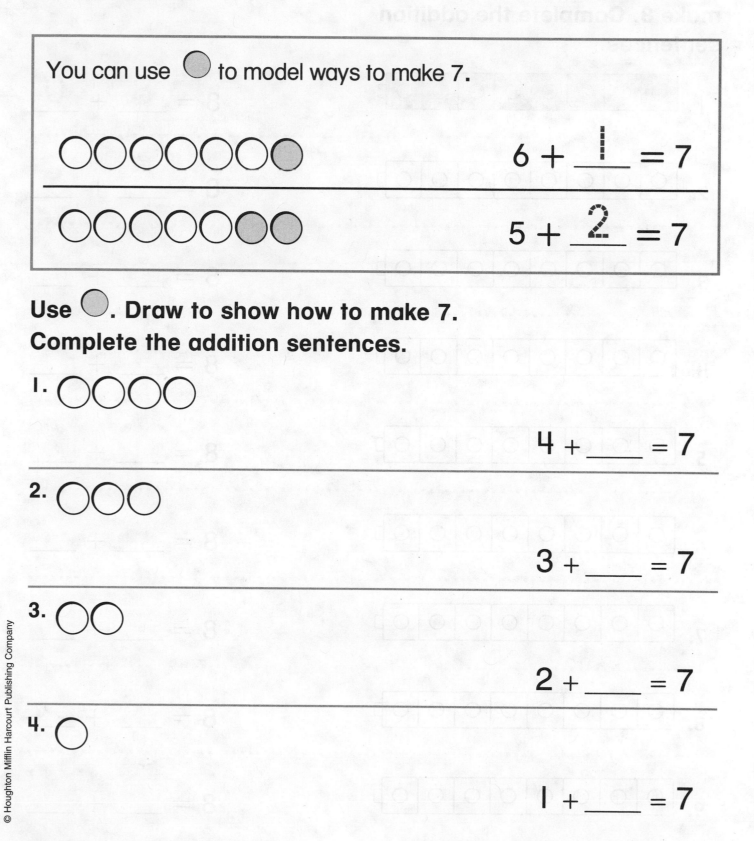

You can use ⬤ to model ways to make 7.

$6 + \underline{1} = 7$

$5 + \underline{2} = 7$

Use ⬤. Draw to show how to make 7.
Complete the addition sentences.

1. ◯◯◯◯ $4 + \underline{\quad} = 7$

2. ◯◯◯ $3 + \underline{\quad} = 7$

3. ◯◯ $2 + \underline{\quad} = 7$

4. ◯ $1 + \underline{\quad} = 7$

Operations and Algebraic Thinking

Algebra • Put Together Numbers to 10

Use 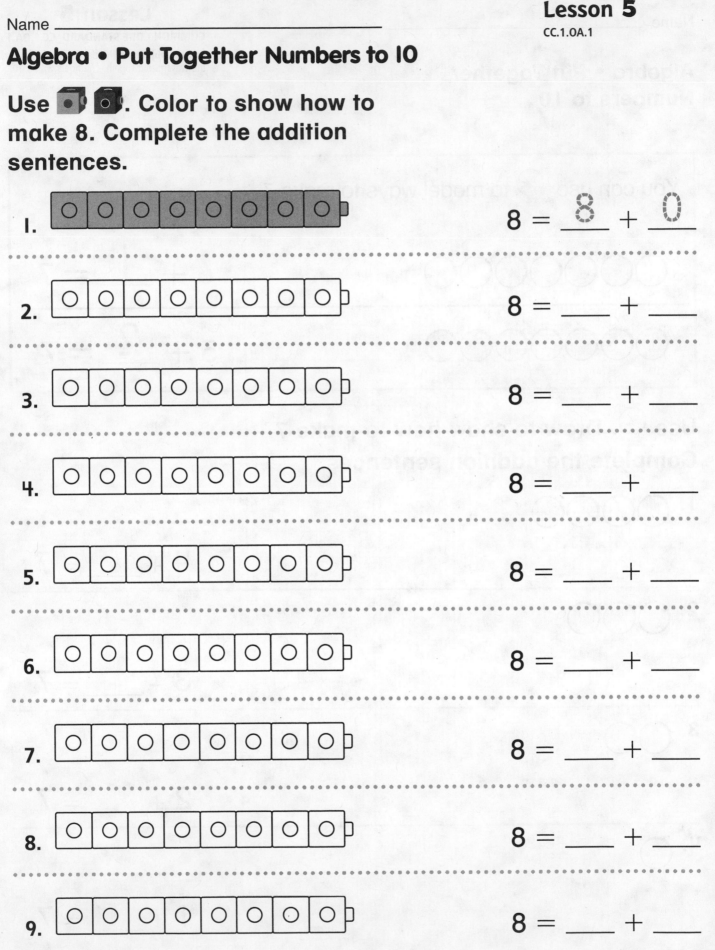 . Color to show how to make 8. Complete the addition sentences.

1. $8 = \underline{8} + \underline{0}$

2. $8 = \underline{} + \underline{}$

3. $8 = \underline{} + \underline{}$

4. $8 = \underline{} + \underline{}$

5. $8 = \underline{} + \underline{}$

6. $8 = \underline{} + \underline{}$

7. $8 = \underline{} + \underline{}$

8. $8 = \underline{} + \underline{}$

9. $8 = \underline{} + \underline{}$

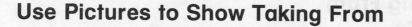

Use Pictures to Show Taking From

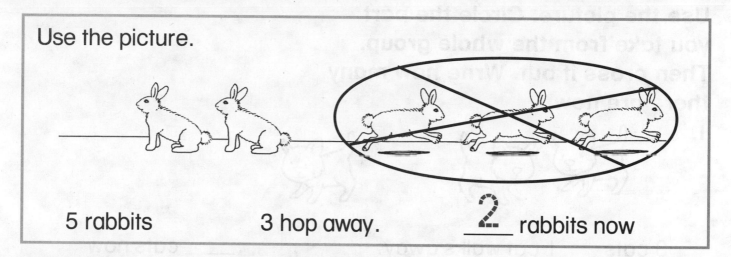

Use the picture.

5 rabbits   3 hop away.   __2__ rabbits now

Write how many there are now.

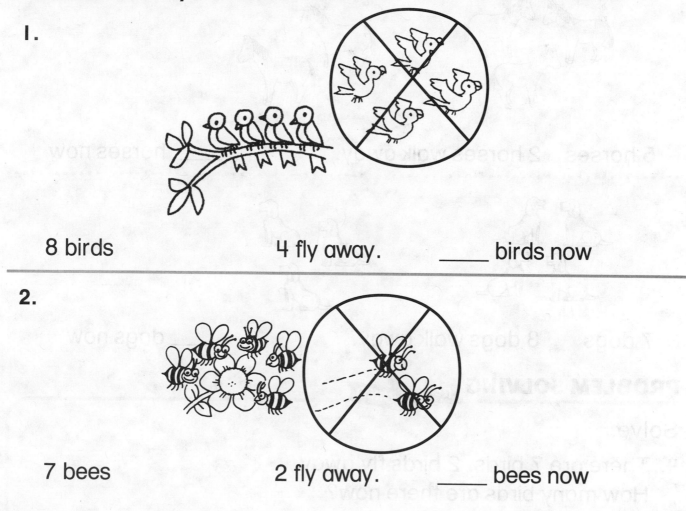

1.

8 birds   4 fly away.   ____ birds now

2.

7 bees   2 fly away.   ____ bees now

Operations and Algebraic Thinking

Use Pictures to Show Taking From

Use the picture. Circle the part you take from the whole group. Then cross it out. Write how many there are now.

1.

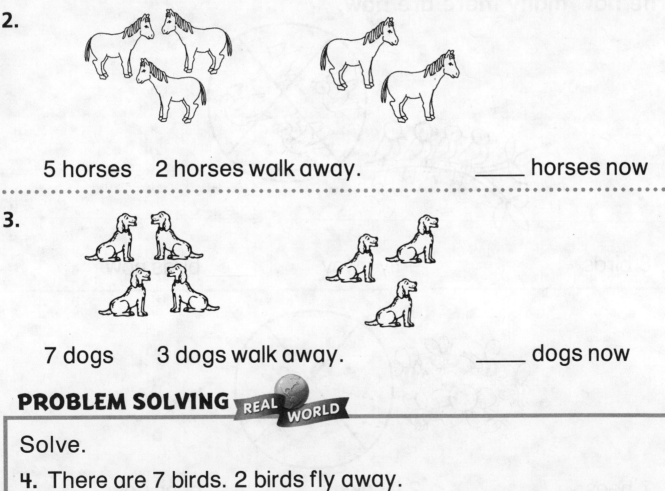

3 cats   I cat walks away.   ____ cats now

2.

5 horses   2 horses walk away.   ____ horses now

3.

7 dogs   3 dogs walk away.   ____ dogs now

PROBLEM SOLVING REAL WORLD

Solve.

4. There are 7 birds. 2 birds fly away. How many birds are there now?

____ birds

Model Taking From

Circle the part you take from the group.
Then cross it out.

3 dogs   2 dogs run away.   _I_ dog now

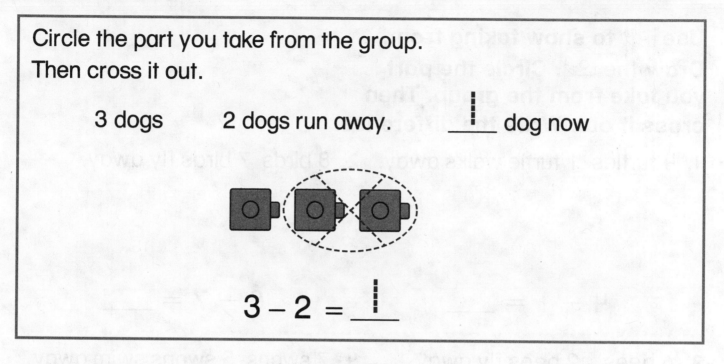

$$3 - 2 = \underline{I}$$

**Circle the part you take from the group.
Then cross it out. Write the difference.**

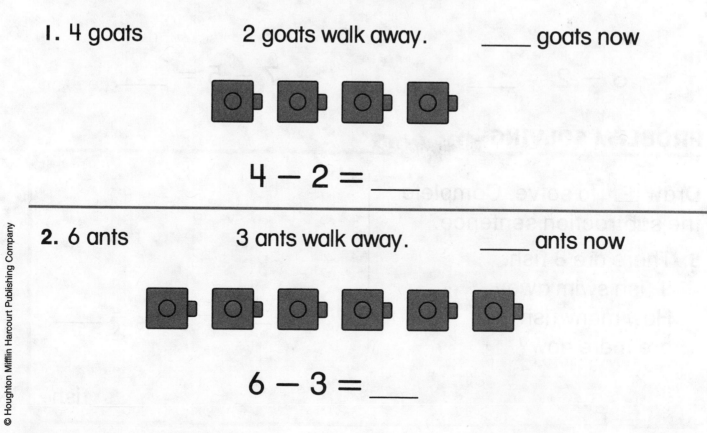

1. 4 goats   2 goats walk away.   ____ goats now

$$4 - 2 = \underline{}$$

2. 6 ants   3 ants walk away.   ____ ants now

$$6 - 3 = \underline{}$$

Model Taking From

Use [die] to show taking from.
Draw the [die]. Circle the part
you take from the group. Then
cross it out. Write the difference.

1. 4 turtles 1 turtle walks away.

2. 8 birds 7 birds fly away.

$$4 - 1 = \underline{\quad}$$

$$8 - 7 = \underline{\quad}$$

3. 6 bees 2 bees fly away.

4. 7 swans 5 swans swim away.

$$6 - 2 = \underline{\quad}$$

$$7 - 5 = \underline{\quad}$$

PROBLEM SOLVING REAL WORLD

Draw [die] to solve. Complete
the subtraction sentence.

5. There are 8 fish.
4 fish swim away.
How many fish
are there now?

$$\underline{\quad} - \underline{\quad} = \underline{\quad}$$

_____ fish

Name _____

Lesson **8**

COMMON CORE STANDARD CC.1.OA.1

Lesson Objective: Use concrete objects to solve "taking apart" subtraction problems.

Model Taking Apart

You can use ◯ to **subtract**.
Sam has 6 cars. 4 cars are red.
The rest are yellow.
How many cars are yellow?

_2_ cars are yellow.

⬤ ⬤ ⬤ ⬤ ◯ ◯

6 − 4 = 2

Use ◯ to solve. Color. Write the number sentence and how many.

1. There are 5 books.
I book is red. The rest are yellow. How many books are yellow?

◯ ◯ ◯ ◯ ◯

___ ◯ ___ ◯ ___

___ yellow books

---

2. There are 6 blocks.
3 blocks are small.
The rest are big.
How many blocks are big?

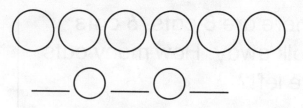

___ ◯ ___ ◯ ___

___ big blocks

Model Taking Apart

Use ⬤ to solve. Draw to show your work. Write the number sentence and how many.

1. There are 7 bags. 2 bags are big. The rest are small. How many bags are small?

    ____ small bags   ___ ◯ ___ ◯ ___

2. There are 6 dogs. 4 dogs are brown. The rest are black. How many dogs are black?

    ____ black dogs   ___ ◯ ___ ◯ ___

PROBLEM SOLVING · REAL WORLD

Solve. Draw a model to explain.

3. There are 8 cats. 6 cats walk away. How many cats are left?

    ____ cats left

Problem Solving • Model Subtraction

There were 9 bugs on a rock. 7 bugs ran away.
How many bugs are on the rock now?

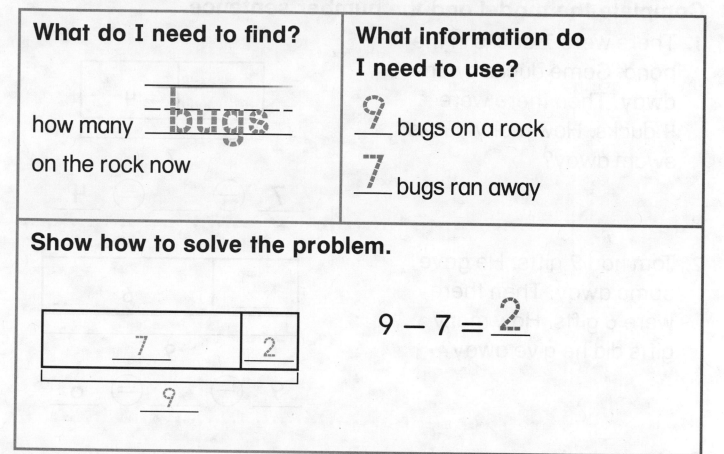

What do I need to find?

how many _bugs_

on the rock now

What information do I need to use?

9 bugs on a rock

7 bugs ran away

Show how to solve the problem.

7	2

9

$9 - 7 = \underline{2}$

Read the problem. Use the model to solve.
Complete the model and the number sentence.

1. There are 5 birds. 1 bird is
   big. The rest are small.
   How many birds are small?

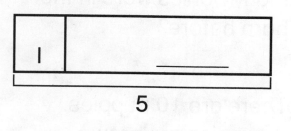

1	

5

$5 - 1 = \underline{}$

Problem Solving • Model Subtraction

Read the problem. Use the model to solve.
Complete the model and the number sentence.

1. There were 7 ducks in the pond. Some ducks swam away. Then there were 4 ducks. How many ducks swam away?

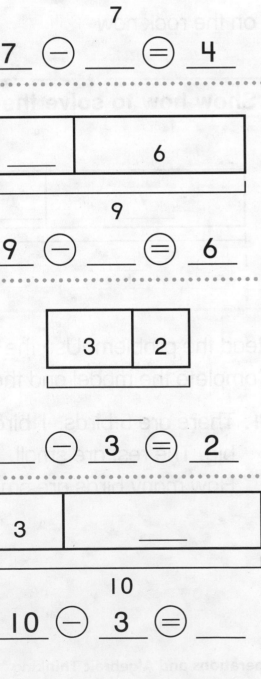

	4

7

7 ⊖ ___ ⊜ 4

2. Tom had 9 gifts. He gave some away. Then there were 6 gifts. How many gifts did he give away?

	6

9

9 ⊖ ___ ⊜ 6

3. Some ponies were in a barn. 3 ponies walked out. Then there were 2 ponies. How many ponies were in the barn before?

3	2

___ ⊖ 3 ⊜ 2

4. There are 10 puppies. 3 puppies are brown. The rest are black. How many puppies are black?

3	

10

10 ⊖ 3 ⊜ ___

Name _____

Lesson 10
COMMON CORE STANDARD CC.1.0A.1
Lesson Objective: Model and compare groups to show the meaning of subtraction.

Subtract to Compare

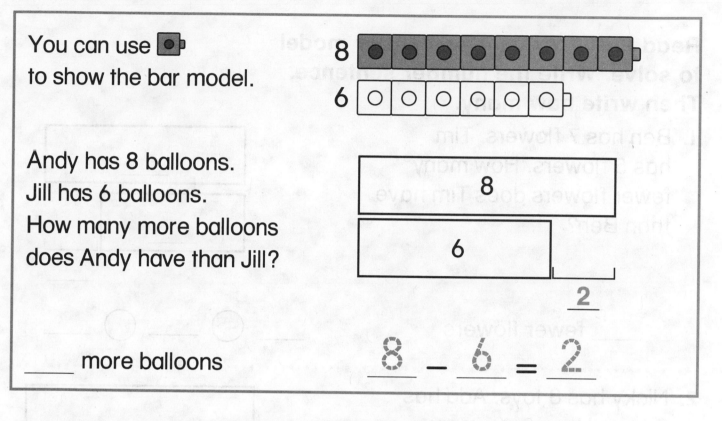

You can use 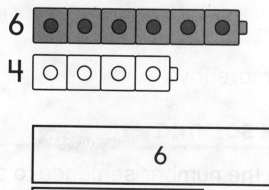 to show the bar model.

8
6

Andy has 8 balloons.
Jill has 6 balloons.
How many more balloons
does Andy have than Jill?

8
6
2

____ more balloons

8 − 6 = 2

Read the problem. Use the bar model to solve. Write the number sentence. Then write how many.

1. Bo has 6 rocks.
   Jen has 4 rocks.
   How many more rocks
   does Bo have than Jen?

6
4

6
4

____ more rocks

___ − ___ = ___

Name _____

Subtract to Compare

Read the problem. Use the bar model to solve. Write the number sentence. Then write how many.

1. Ben has 7 flowers. Tim has 5 flowers. How many fewer flowers does Tim have than Ben?

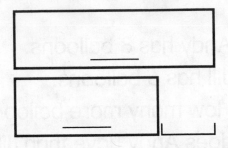

_____ fewer flowers

_____ ◯ _____ ◯ _____

2. Nicky has 8 toys. Ada has 3 toys. How many more toys does Nicky have than Ada?

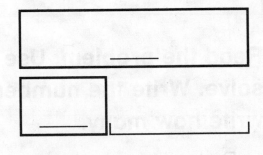

_____ more toys

_____ ◯ _____ ◯ _____

PROBLEM SOLVING REAL WORLD

Complete the number sentence to solve.

3. Maya has 7 pens. Sam has 1 pen. How many more pens does Maya have than Sam?

_____ − _____ = _____

_____ more pens

Algebra • Take Apart Numbers

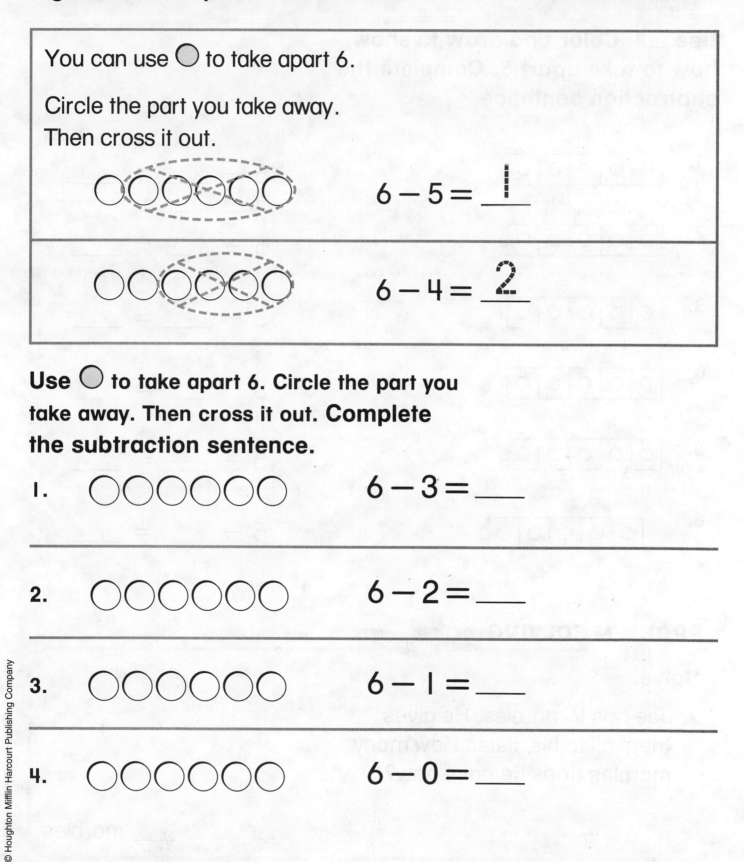

You can use ◯ to take apart 6.

Circle the part you take away.
Then cross it out.

$6 - 5 =$ __1__

$6 - 4 =$ __2__

Use ◯ **to take apart 6. Circle the part you take away. Then cross it out. Complete the subtraction sentence.**

1. $6 - 3 =$ ___

2. $6 - 2 =$ ___

3. $6 - 1 =$ ___

4. $6 - 0 =$ ___

Algebra • Take Apart Numbers

Use ⬚. Color and draw to show how to take apart 5. Complete the subtraction sentence.

1. ☐☐☐☐☐   5 − ___ = ___

2. ☐☐☐☐☐   5 − ___ = ___

3. ☐☐☐☐☐   5 − ___ = ___

4. ☐☐☐☐☐   5 − ___ = ___

5. ☐☐☐☐☐   5 − ___ = ___

6. ☐☐☐☐☐   5 − ___ = ___

PROBLEM SOLVING REAL WORLD

Solve.

7. Joe has 9 marbles. He gives them all to his sister. How many marbles does he have now?

_____ marbles

Problem Solving • Use Subtraction Strategies

Lara has 15 crackers. She gives
some of them away. She has 8 left.
How many crackers does she give away?

Unlock the Problem

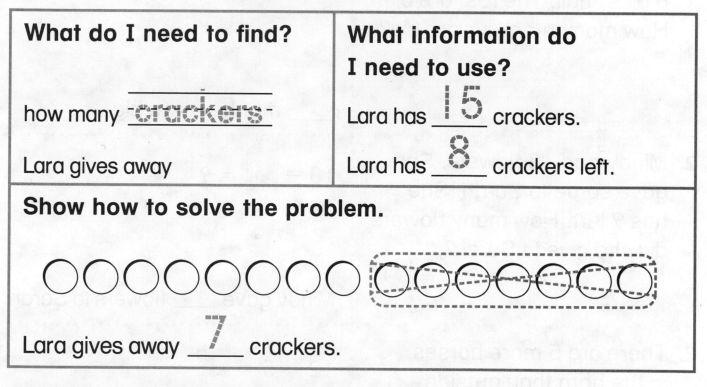

What do I need to find?	**What information do I need to use?**
how many ~~crackers~~	Lara has __15__ crackers.
Lara gives away	Lara has __8__ crackers left.

Show how to solve the problem.

Lara gives away __7__ crackers.

Act it out to solve. Draw to show your work.

1. Min has 13 marbles.
   She gives some away.
   She has 5 left.
   How many marbles does
   she give away?

   Min gives away _____ marbles.

Operations and Algebraic Thinking

Problem Solving • Use Subtraction Strategies

Act it out to solve.
Draw to show your work.

1. There are 13 monkeys.
6 are small. The rest are big.
How many monkeys are big?

$13 - 6 =$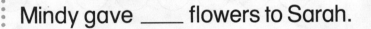

____ monkeys are big.

2. Mindy had 13 flowers. She
gave some to Sarah. She
has 9 left. How many flowers
did she give to Sarah?

$13 -$ ▢ $= 9$

Mindy gave ____ flowers to Sarah.

3. There are 5 more horses
in the barn than outside.
12 horses are in the barn.
How many horses are
outside?

$12 - 5 =$ ▢

____ horses are outside.

4. Kim has 15 pennies.
John has 6 pennies.
How many fewer pennies
does John have than Kim?

$15 - 6 =$ ▢

John has ____ fewer pennies.

Name _____

Lesson 13

COMMON CORE STANDARD CC.1.OA.1

Lesson Objective: Solve addition and subtraction problem situations using the strategy *make a model*.

Problem Solving • Add or Subtract

There are 12 skunks in the woods.

Some skunks walk away.

There are 8 skunks still in the woods.

How many skunks walk away?

Unlock the Problem

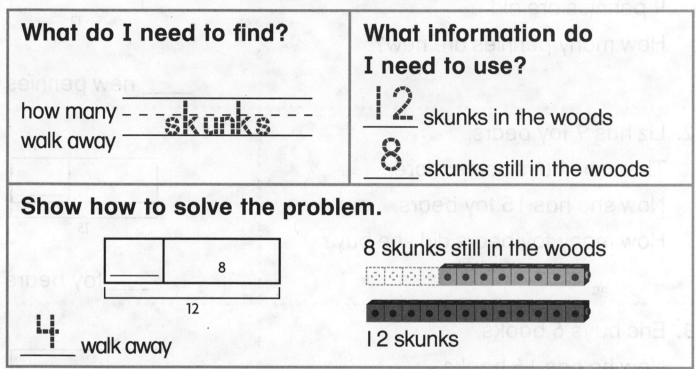

What do I need to find?	**What information do I need to use?**
how many walk away - - - skunks - - -	12 skunks in the woods 8 skunks still in the woods

Show how to solve the problem.

8

12

4 walk away

8 skunks still in the woods

12 skunks

Make a model to solve.

Use 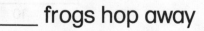 to help you.

1. There are 15 frogs on a log.

Some frogs hop away.

There are 7 frogs still on the log.

How many frogs hop away?

_____ frogs hop away

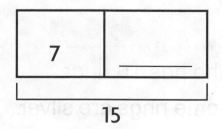

7

15

Add or Subtract

Make a model to solve.

1. Stan has 12 pennies.

   Some pennies are new.

   4 pennies are old.

   How many pennies are new?

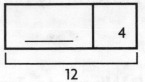

____ new pennies

2. Liz has 9 toy bears.

   Then she buys some more.

   Now she has 15 toy bears.

   How many toy bears did she buy?

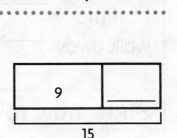

____ toy bears

3. Eric buys 6 books.

   Now he has 16 books.

   How many books did he have to start?

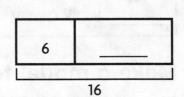

____ books

4. Cho has 10 rings.

   Some rings are silver.

   4 rings are gold.

   How many rings are silver?

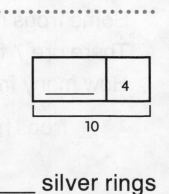

____ silver rings

Choose an Operation

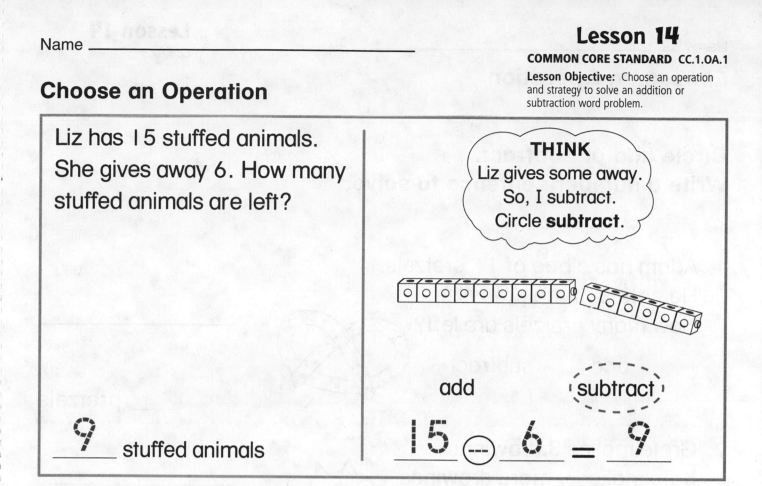

Liz has 15 stuffed animals. She gives away 6. How many stuffed animals are left?

THINK
Liz gives some away.
So, I subtract.
Circle **subtract**.

add   (subtract)

_9_ stuffed animals

15 ⊖ 6 = 9

Circle add or subtract.
Write a number sentence to solve.

1. Misha has 11 crackers.
He eats 2 crackers.
How many crackers are left?

add   subtract

_____ crackers   _____ ◯ _____ = _____

2. Lynn has 5 shells.
Dan has 7 shells.
How many shells do Lynn and Dan have?

add   subtract

_____ shells   _____ ◯ _____ = _____

Choose an Operation

Circle add or subtract.
Write a number sentence to solve.

1. Adam has a bag of 11 pretzels.
   He eats 2 of the pretzels.
   How many pretzels are left?

   add   subtract

   _____

   _____ pretzels

2. Greta makes 3 drawings.
   Kate makes 4 more drawings
   than Greta. How many
   drawings does Kate make?

   add   subtract

   _____

   _____ drawings

PROBLEM SOLVING REAL WORLD

Choose a way to solve.
Write or draw to explain.

3. Greg has 11 shirts.
   3 have long sleeves.
   The rest have short sleeves.
   How many short-sleeve
   shirts does Greg have?

   _____ short-sleeve shirts

Name _____

Lesson 15

COMMON CORE STANDARD CC.1.OA.2

Lesson Objective: Solve adding to and putting together situations using the strategy *draw a picture.*

Problem Solving •
Use Addition Strategies

Tory has 9 toys. Bob has 4 toys.
Joy has 2 toys. How many toys
do they have?

Unlock the Problem

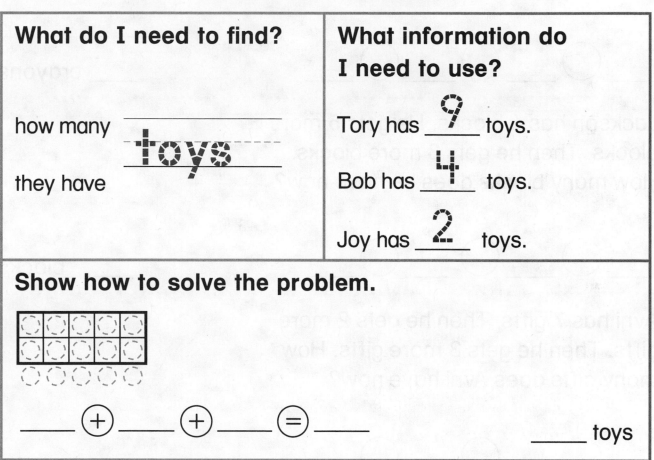

What do I need to find?

how many _____ **toys**

they have

What information do I need to use?

Tory has __9__ toys.

Bob has __4__ toys.

Joy has __2__ toys.

Show how to solve the problem.

____ $+$ ____ $+$ ____ $=$ ____

_____ toys

Draw a picture to solve.

1. Rick has 7 books.
   He gets 2 more books.
   He then gets 2 more books.
   How many books does
   Rick have now?

_____ books

Operations and Algebraic Thinking

© Houghton Mifflin Harcourt Publishing Company

Name _____

Problem Solving • Use Addition Strategies

Draw a picture to solve.

1. Franco has 5 crayons. He gets 8 more crayons. Then he gets 2 more crayons. How many crayons does he have now?

____ ◯ ____ ◯ ____ ◯ ____   ____ crayons

2. Jackson has 6 blocks. He gets 5 more blocks. Then he gets 3 more blocks. How many blocks does he have now?

____ ◯ ____ ◯ ____ ◯ ____   ____ blocks

3. Avni has 7 gifts. Then he gets 2 more gifts. Then he gets 3 more gifts. How many gifts does Avni have now?

____ ◯ ____ ◯ ____ ◯ ____   ____ gifts

4. Meeka has 4 rings. She gets 2 more rings. Then she gets 1 more ring. How many rings does she have now?

____ ◯ ____ ◯ ____ ◯ ____   ____ rings

30

Name _____

Lesson 16
COMMON CORE STANDARD CC.1.OA.3
Lesson Objective: Understand and apply
the Additive Identity Property for Addition.

Algebra • Add Zero

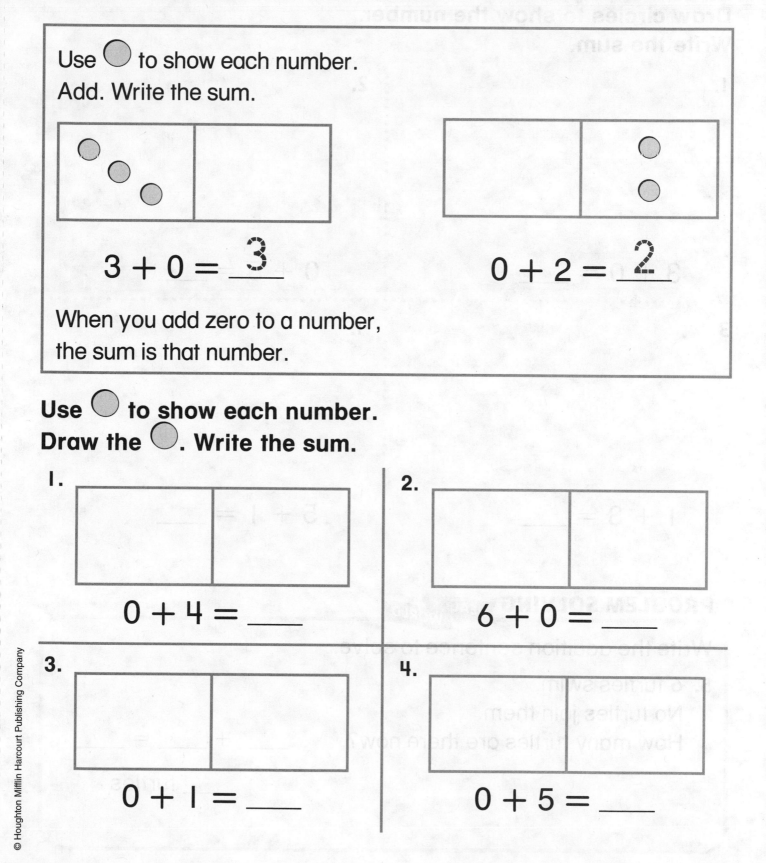

Use ◯ to show each number.
Add. Write the sum.

$3 + 0 = \underline{3}$

$0 + 2 = \underline{2}$

When you add zero to a number,
the sum is that number.

Use ◯ to show each number.
Draw the ◯. Write the sum.

1.

$0 + 4 = \underline{}$

2.

$6 + 0 = \underline{}$

3.

$0 + 1 = \underline{}$

4.

$0 + 5 = \underline{}$

Algebra • Add Zero

Draw circles to show the number.
Write the sum.

1.

$3 + 0 =$ ___

2.

$0 + 5 =$ ___

3.

$1 + 3 =$ ___

4.

$5 + 1 =$ ___

PROBLEM SOLVING

Write the addition sentence to solve.

5. 6 turtles swim.
No turtles join them.
How many turtles are there now?   ___ + ___ = ___

___ turtles

Name _____

Lesson 17
COMMON CORE STANDARD CC.1.OA.3
Lesson Objective: Explore the
Commutative Property of Addition.

Algebra • Add in Any Order

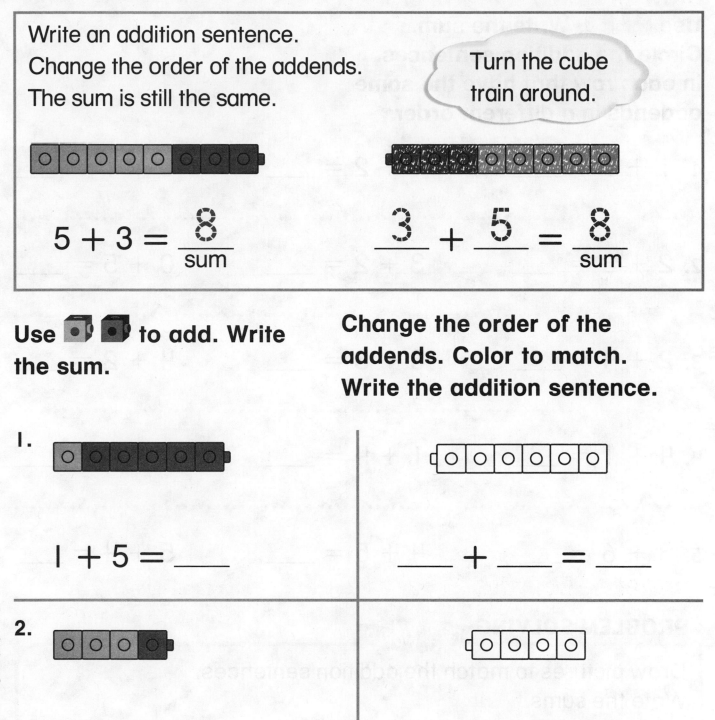

Write an addition sentence.
Change the order of the addends.
The sum is still the same.

Turn the cube
train around.

$5 + 3 = \underline{8}$
sum

$\underline{3} + \underline{5} = \underline{8}$
sum

Use 🎲 🎲 to add. Write
the sum.

Change the order of the
addends. Color to match.
Write the addition sentence.

1.

$1 + 5 = \underline{\quad}$

$\underline{\quad} + \underline{\quad} = \underline{\quad}$

2.

$3 + 1 = \underline{\quad}$

$\underline{\quad} + \underline{\quad} = \underline{\quad}$

Algebra • Add in Any Order

Use 🎲 🎲. Write the sum.
Circle the addition sentences
in each row that have the same
addends in a different order.

1. $1 + 3 =$ ___ $1 + 2 =$ ___ $3 + 1 =$ ___

2. $2 + 3 =$ ___ $3 + 2 =$ ___ $0 + 5 =$ ___

3. $2 + 4 =$ ___ $3 + 3 =$ ___ $4 + 2 =$ ___

4. $4 + 1 =$ ___ $1 + 4 =$ ___ $0 + 4 =$ ___

5. $3 + 6 =$ ___ $4 + 5 =$ ___ $5 + 4 =$ ___

PROBLEM SOLVING REAL WORLD

Draw pictures to match the addition sentences.
Write the sums.

6. $5 + 2 =$ ___

   $2 + 5 =$ ___

Algebra • Add in Any Order

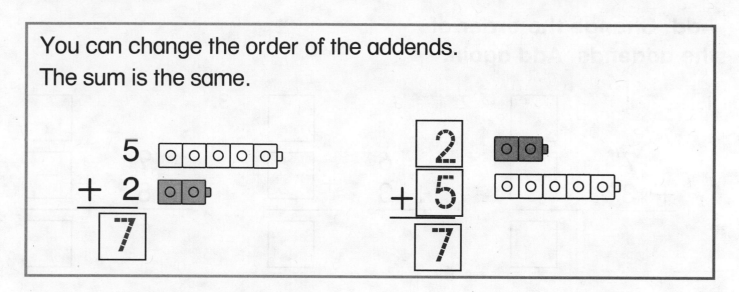

You can change the order of the addends.
The sum is the same.

Add. Change the order of the addends. Add again.

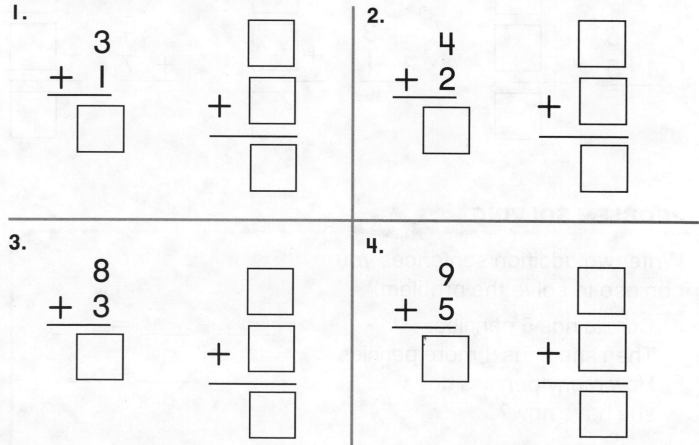

1.

$$\begin{array}{r} 3 \\ + 1 \\ \hline \end{array}$$

2.

$$\begin{array}{r} 4 \\ + 2 \\ \hline \end{array}$$

3.

$$\begin{array}{r} 8 \\ + 3 \\ \hline \end{array}$$

4.

$$\begin{array}{r} 9 \\ + 5 \\ \hline \end{array}$$

Algebra • Add in Any Order

**Add. Change the order of
the addends. Add again.**

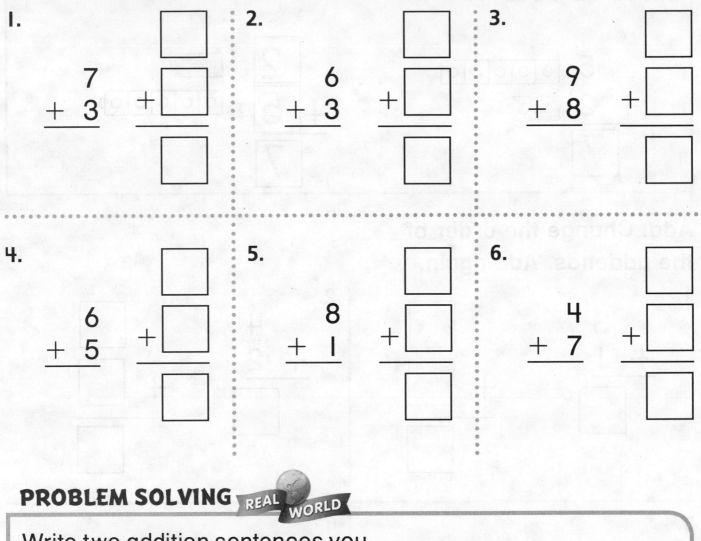

1.
$$\begin{array}{r} 7 \\ + 3 \\ \hline \end{array}$$
☐
+ ☐
☐

2.
$$\begin{array}{r} 6 \\ + 3 \\ \hline \end{array}$$
☐
+ ☐
☐

3.
$$\begin{array}{r} 9 \\ + 8 \\ \hline \end{array}$$
☐
+ ☐
☐

4.
$$\begin{array}{r} 6 \\ + 5 \\ \hline \end{array}$$
☐
+ ☐
☐

5.
$$\begin{array}{r} 8 \\ + 1 \\ \hline \end{array}$$
☐
+ ☐
☐

6.
$$\begin{array}{r} 4 \\ + 7 \\ \hline \end{array}$$
☐
+ ☐
☐

PROBLEM SOLVING 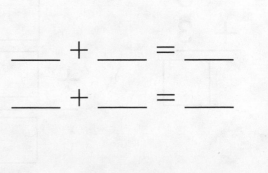 REAL WORLD

Write two addition sentences you
can use to solve the problem.

7. Camila has 5 pennies.
Then she finds 4 more pennies.
How many pennies does
she have now?

___ + ___ = ___

___ + ___ = ___

Name _____

Lesson 19

COMMON CORE STANDARD CC.1.OA.3

Lesson Objective: Use the Associative Property of Addition to add three addends.

Algebra • Add 3 Numbers

You can add numbers in any order.

$3 + 4 + 1 = 8$

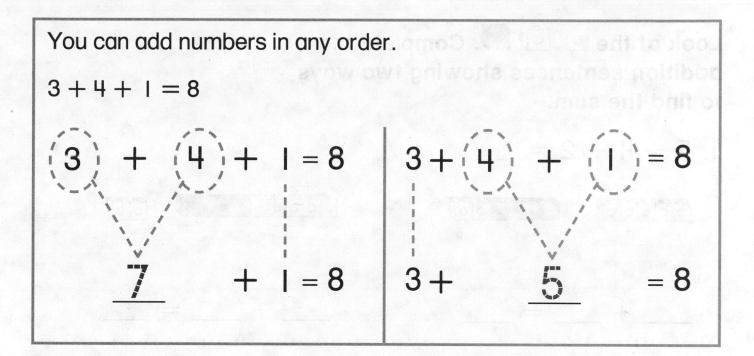

Use circles to change which two addends you add first. Complete the addition sentences.

1.

$\textcircled{2} + \textcircled{1} + 8 = 11$

___ $+ 8 = 11$

$2 + \textcircled{1} + \textcircled{8} = 11$

$2 +$ ___ $= 11$

2.

$\textcircled{7} + \textcircled{2} + 3 = 12$

___ $+ 3 = 12$

$7 + \textcircled{2} + \textcircled{3} = 12$

$7 +$ ___ $= 12$

Algebra • Add 3 Numbers

Look at the 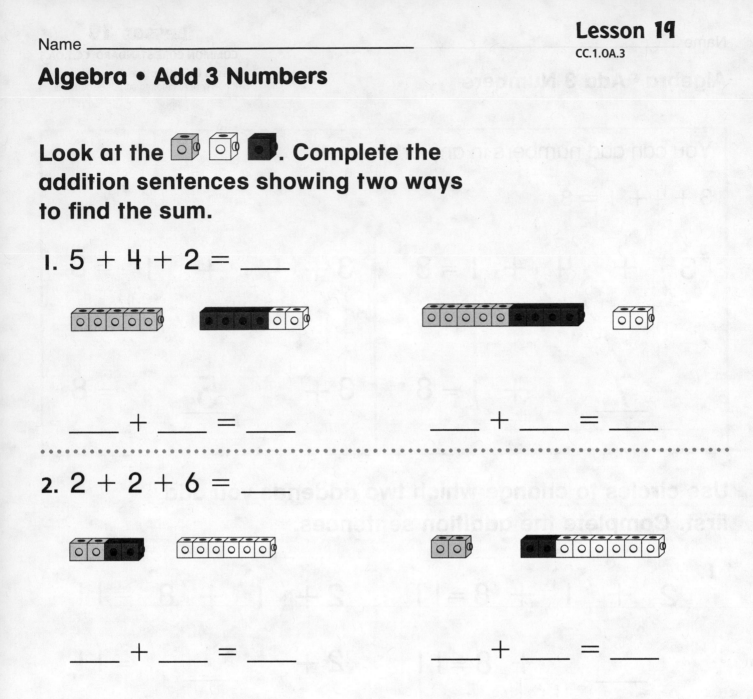. Complete the
addition sentences showing two ways
to find the sum.

1. $5 + 4 + 2 =$ ___

___ + ___ = ___   ___ + ___ = ___

2. $2 + 2 + 6 =$ ___

___ + ___ = ___   ___ + ___ = ___

PROBLEM SOLVING

3. Choose three numbers from 1 to 6.
   Write the numbers in an addition sentence.
   Show two ways to find the sum.

Algebra • Add 3 Numbers

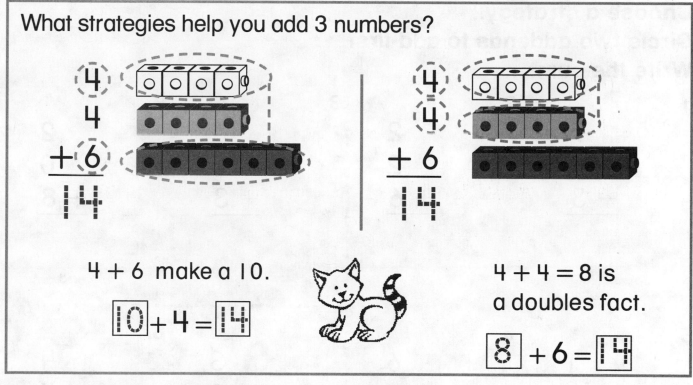

What strategies help you add 3 numbers?

4 + 6 make a 10.

$\boxed{10} + 4 = \boxed{14}$

$4 + 4 = 8$ is a doubles fact.

$\boxed{8} + 6 = \boxed{14}$

Choose a strategy. Circle two addends to add first. Write the sum.
Then find the total sum.

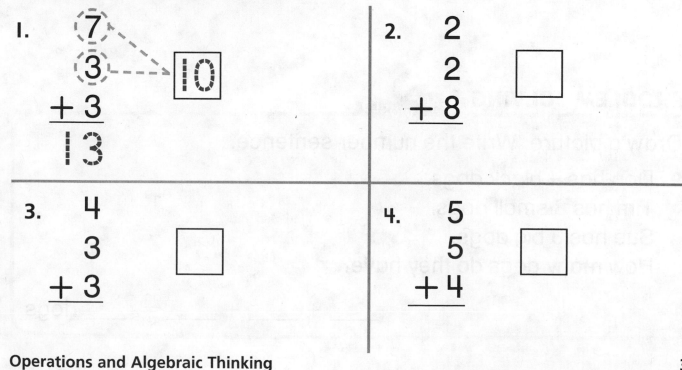

1. 7
   3     $\boxed{10}$
   + 3
   13

2. 2
   2     $\boxed{}$
   + 8

3. 4
   3     $\boxed{}$
   + 3

4. 5
   5     $\boxed{}$
   + 4

Algebra • Add 3 Numbers

Choose a strategy.
Circle two addends to add first.
Write the sum.

1.
```
  7
  3
+ 3
____
```

2.
```
  2
  2
+ 6
____
```

3.
```
  6
  6
+ 3
____
```

4.
```
  2
  0
+ 8
____
```

5.
```
  1
  2
+ 9
____
```

6.
```
  6
  4
+ 3
____
```

7.
```
  3
  3
+ 5
____
```

8.
```
  4
  4
+ 8
____
```

PROBLEM SOLVING REAL WORLD

Draw a picture. Write the number sentence.

9. Don has 4 black dogs.
   Tim has 3 small dogs.
   Sue has 3 big dogs.
   How many dogs do they have?

____ + ____ + ____ = ____ dogs

Think Addition to Subtract

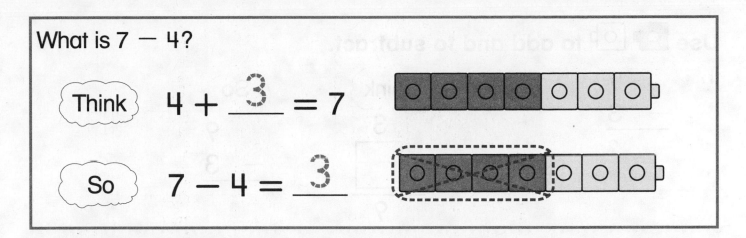

What is 7 − 4?

Think   4 + __3__ = 7

So   7 − 4 = __3__

Use 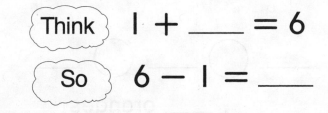 to model the number sentences.
Draw to show your work.

1. What is 11 − 2?

Think   2 + ___ = 11

So   11 − 2 = ___

2. What is 10 − 6?

Think   6 + ___ = 10

So   10 − 6 = ___

3. What is 6 − 1?

Think   1 + ___ = 6

So   6 − 1 = ___

Operations and Algebraic Thinking

Think Addition to Subtract

Use 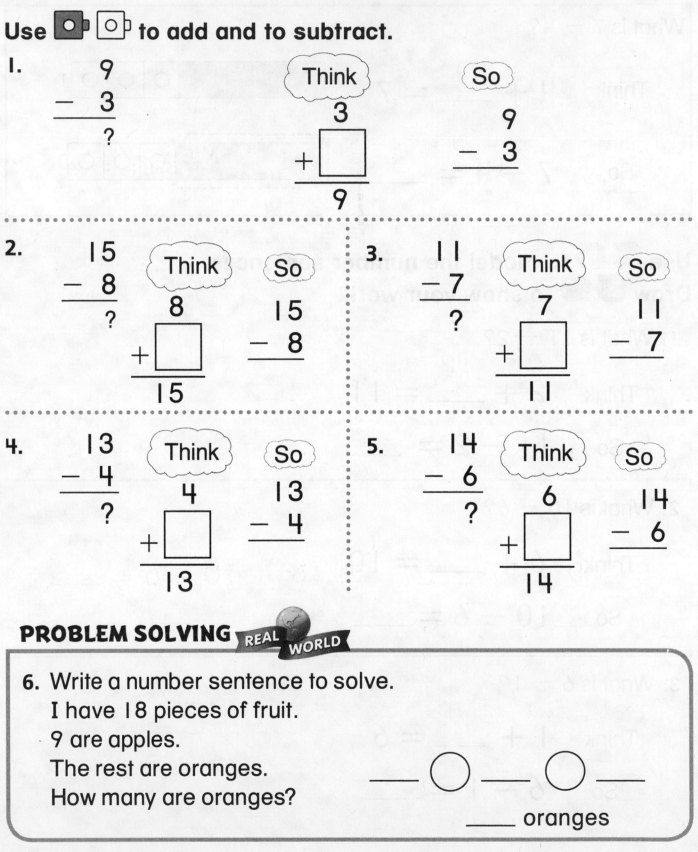 to add and to subtract.

1.
   9
  − 3
  ___
   ?

   Think
   3
   +☐
   ___
   9

   So
   9
   − 3
   ___

2.
   15
  − 8
  ___
   ?

   Think
   8
   +☐
   ___
   15

   So
   15
   − 8
   ___

3.
   11
  − 7
  ___
   ?

   Think
   7
   +☐
   ___
   11

   So
   11
   − 7
   ___

4.
   13
  − 4
  ___
   ?

   Think
   4
   +☐
   ___
   13

   So
   13
   − 4
   ___

5.
   14
  − 6
  ___
   ?

   Think
   6
   +☐
   ___
   14

   So
   14
   − 6
   ___

PROBLEM SOLVING REAL WORLD

6. Write a number sentence to solve.
   I have 18 pieces of fruit.
   9 are apples.
   The rest are oranges.
   How many are oranges?

   ____ ◯ ____ ◯ ____

   ____ oranges

Use Think Addition to Subtract

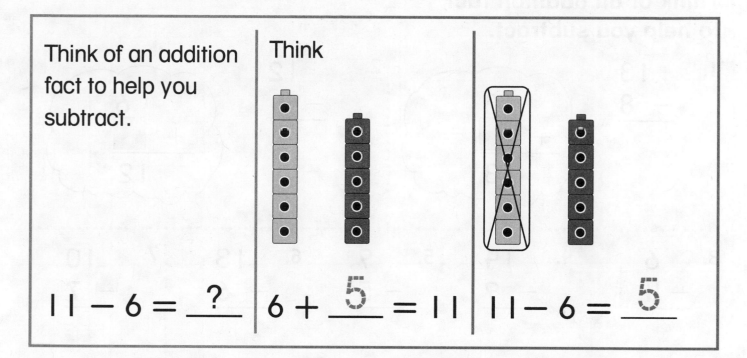

Think of an addition fact to help you subtract.

Think

$11 - 6 = \underline{\quad ?\quad}$

$6 + \underline{\quad 5\quad} = 11$

$11 - 6 = \underline{\quad 5\quad}$

Use an addition fact to help you subtract.

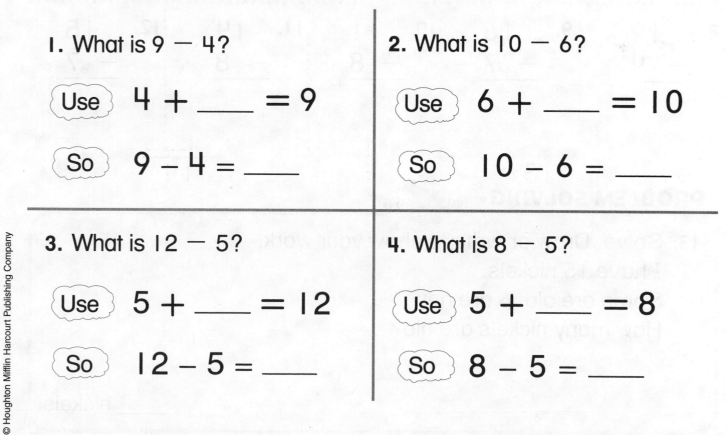

1. What is $9 - 4$?

Use $4 + \underline{\quad} = 9$

So $9 - 4 = \underline{\quad}$

2. What is $10 - 6$?

Use $6 + \underline{\quad} = 10$

So $10 - 6 = \underline{\quad}$

3. What is $12 - 5$?

Use $5 + \underline{\quad} = 12$

So $12 - 5 = \underline{\quad}$

4. What is $8 - 5$?

Use $5 + \underline{\quad} = 8$

So $8 - 5 = \underline{\quad}$

Name _____

Use Think Addition to Subtract

Think of an addition fact to help you subtract.

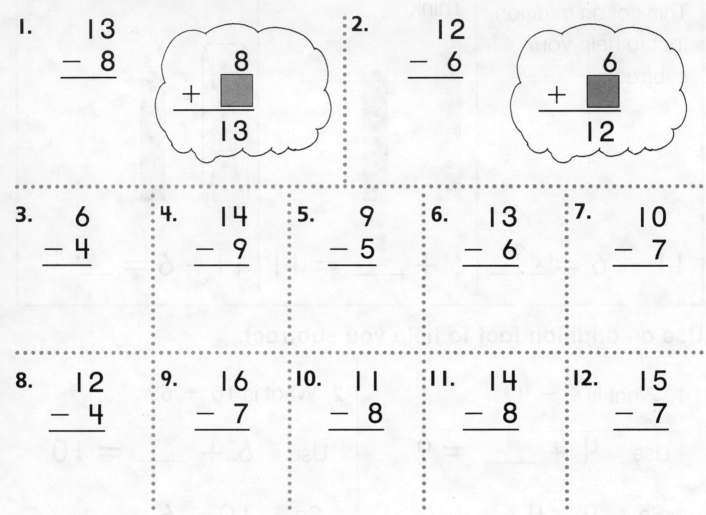

1.   13
   − 8

   8
 + ☐
 ─────
   13

2.   12
   − 6

   6
 + ☐
 ─────
   12

3.   6
   − 4

4.   14
   − 9

5.   9
   − 5

6.   13
   − 6

7.   10
   − 7

8.   12
   − 4

9.   16
   − 7

10.   11
    − 8

11.   14
    − 8

12.   15
    − 7

PROBLEM SOLVING REAL WORLD

13. Solve. Draw or write to show your work.
    I have 15 nickels.
    Some are old. 6 are new.
    How many nickels are old?

    _____ nickels

Lesson 23

COMMON CORE STANDARD CC.1.OA.5

Lesson Objective: Use count on 1, 2, or 3 as a strategy to find sums within 20.

Name _____

Count On

You can count on to find $4 + 3$.
Start with the greater addend.
Then count on. Write the sum.

To add 3,
count on 3.

4   ◯5   ◯6   ◯7

$4 + 3 = \underline{7}$

Circle the greater addend. Count on 1, 2, or 3.
Write the missing numbers.

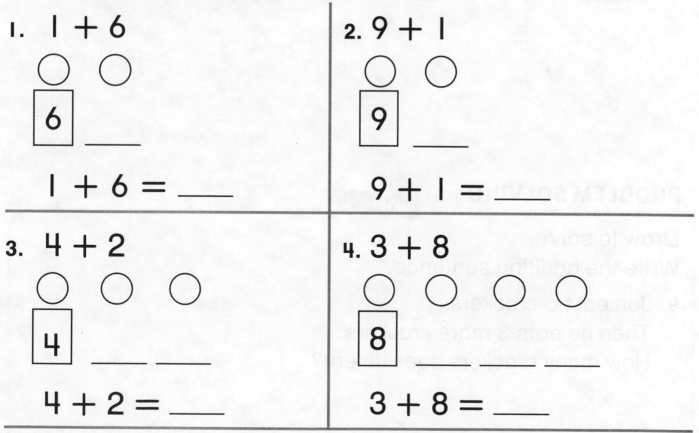

1. $1 + 6$

◯ ◯

6 ___

$1 + 6 = \underline{}$

2. $9 + 1$

◯ ◯

9 ___

$9 + 1 = \underline{}$

3. $4 + 2$

◯ ◯ ◯

4 ___ ___

$4 + 2 = \underline{}$

4. $3 + 8$

◯ ◯ ◯ ◯

8 ___

$3 + 8 = \underline{}$

Operations and Algebraic Thinking

Count On

Circle the greater addend.
Count on to find the sum.

1. 8
   + 2

2. 1
   + 7

3. 3
   + 9

4. 5
   + 3

5. 7
   + 3

6. 3
   + 4

7. 6
   + 2

8. 1
   + 8

PROBLEM SOLVING REAL WORLD

Draw to solve.
Write the addition sentence.

9. Jon eats 6 crackers.
   Then he eats 3 more crackers.
   How many crackers does he eat?

   ____ + ____ = ____ crackers

Name _____

Lesson 24
COMMON CORE STANDARD CC.1.OA.5
Lesson Objective: Use count back
1, 2, or 3 as a strategy to subtract.

Count Back

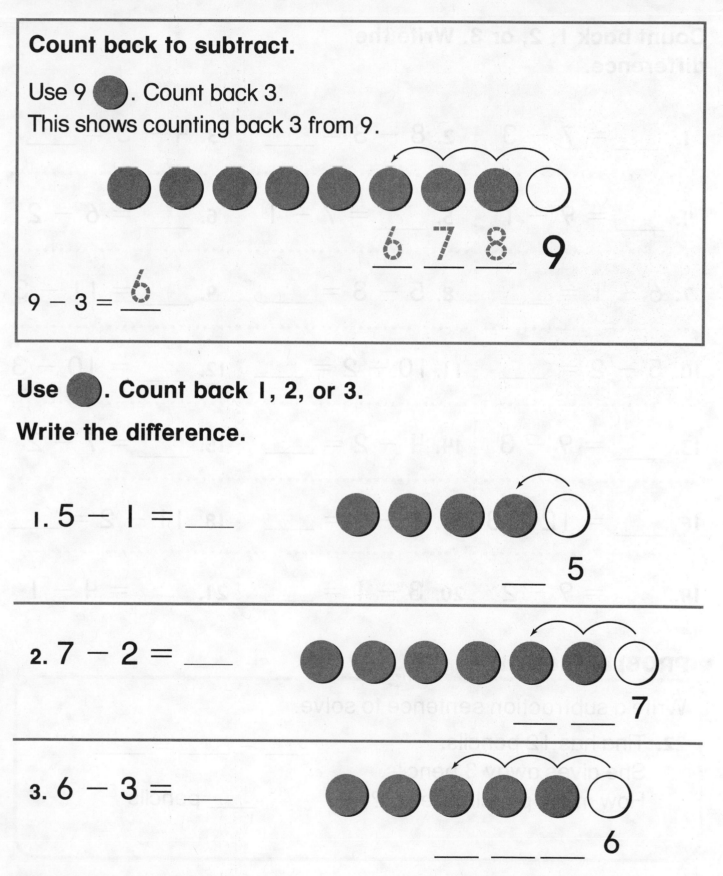

Count back to subtract.

Use 9 ⬤. Count back 3.

This shows counting back 3 from 9.

6 7 8 9

$9 - 3 = \underline{6}$

Use ⬤. Count back 1, 2, or 3.

Write the difference.

1. $5 - 1 = \underline{}$

___ 5

2. $7 - 2 = \underline{}$

___ ___ 7

3. $6 - 3 = \underline{}$

___ ___ 6

Count Back

Count back 1, 2, or 3. Write the difference.

1. ___ = 7 − 3

2. 8 − 3 = ___

3. 4 − 3 = ___

4. ___ = 9 − 1

5. ___ = 7 − 1

6. ___ = 6 − 2

7. 6 − 1 = ___

8. 5 − 3 = ___

9. ___ = 11 − 3

10. 5 − 2 = ___

11. 10 − 2 = ___

12. ___ = 10 − 3

13. ___ = 9 − 3

14. 4 − 2 = ___

15. ___ = 7 − 2

16. ___ = 12 − 3

17. 8 − 1 = ___

18. 11 − 2 = ___

19. ___ = 9 − 2

20. 3 − 1 = ___

21. ___ = 4 − 1

PROBLEM SOLVING REAL WORLD

Write a subtraction sentence to solve.

22. Tina has 12 pencils.
She gives away 3 pencils.
How many pencils are left?

___ − ___ = ___

____ pencils

Name _____

Lesson 25
COMMON CORE STANDARD CC.1.OA.6
Lesson Objective: Build fluency for addition within 10.

Addition to 10

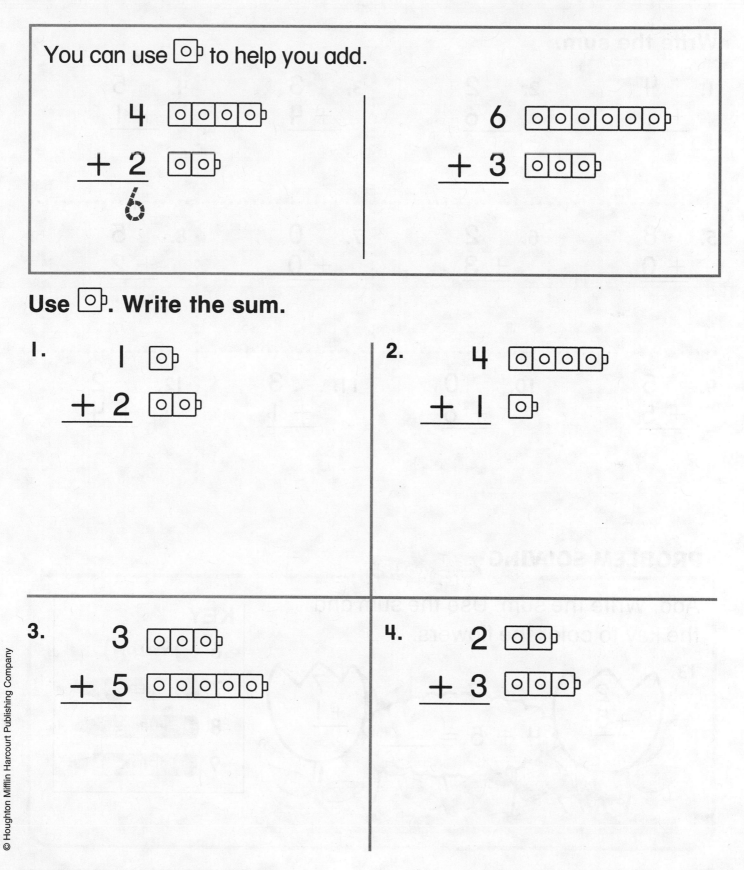

You can use ▢ to help you add.

$$4 + 2 = 6$$

$$6 + 3 =$$

Use ▢. Write the sum.

1.
$$1 + 2 =$$

2.
$$4 + 1 =$$

3.
$$3 + 5 =$$

4.
$$2 + 3 =$$

Operations and Algebraic Thinking

Addition to 10

Write the sum.

1. 4
   +1

2. 2
   +6

3. 3
   +4

4. 5
   +1

5. 8
   +0

6. 2
   +3

7. 0
   +0

8. 5
   +2

9. 5
   +5

10. 0
    +6

11. 3
    +1

12. 2
    +4

PROBLEM SOLVING REAL WORLD

Add. Write the sum. Use the sum and the key to color the flowers.

13.

2
+5

4 + 5 = ___

7
+1

KEY

6 YELLOW

7 RED

8 PURPLE

9 PINK

Name _____

Subtraction from 10 or Less

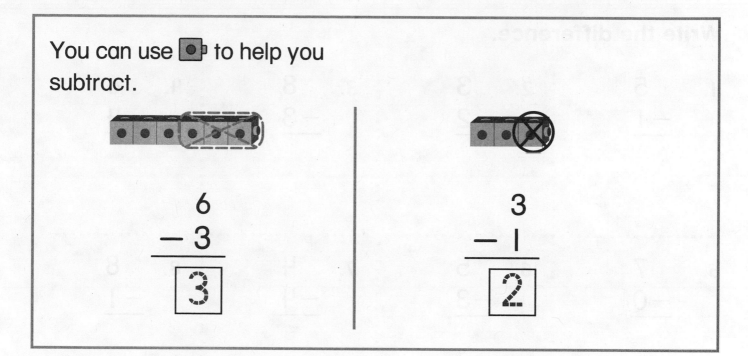

You can use ■ to help you subtract.

6
−3
[3]

3
−1
[2]

Write the subtraction problem.

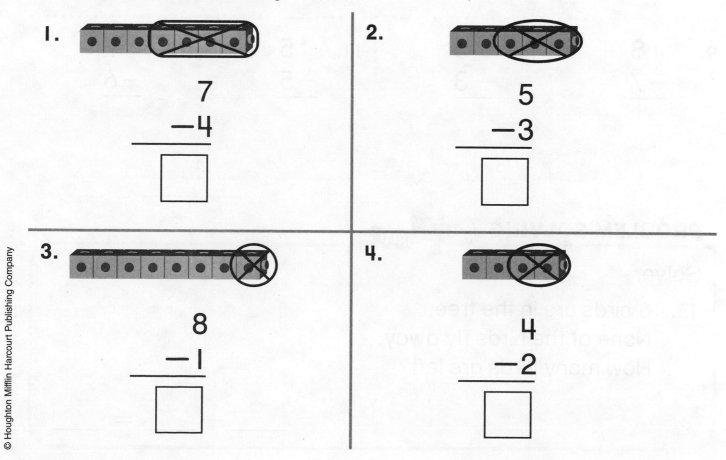

1.
7
−4
☐

2.
5
−3
☐

3.
8
−1
☐

4.
4
−2
☐

Operations and Algebraic Thinking

Subraction from 10 or Less

Write the difference.

1.   5
   −1

2.   3
   −2

3.   8
   −3

4.   6
   −4

5.   7
   −0

6.   5
   −3

7.   4
   −4

8.   8
   −1

9.   8
   −7

10.   6
   −3

11.   5
   −5

12.   7
   −6

PROBLEM SOLVING REAL WORLD

Solve.

13. 6 birds are in the tree.
   None of the birds fly away.
   How many birds are left?

   ___ − ___ = ___

Name _____

Lesson 27
COMMON CORE STANDARD CC.1.OA.6
Lesson Objective: Use doubles as a strategy to solve addition facts with sums within 20.

Add Doubles

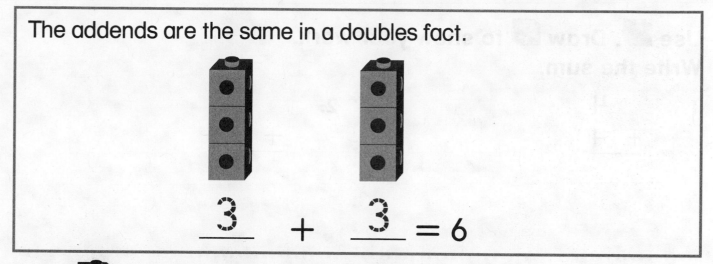

The addends are the same in a doubles fact.

__3__ + __3__ = 6

Draw 🔲 **to show the addends.**
Write the missing numbers.

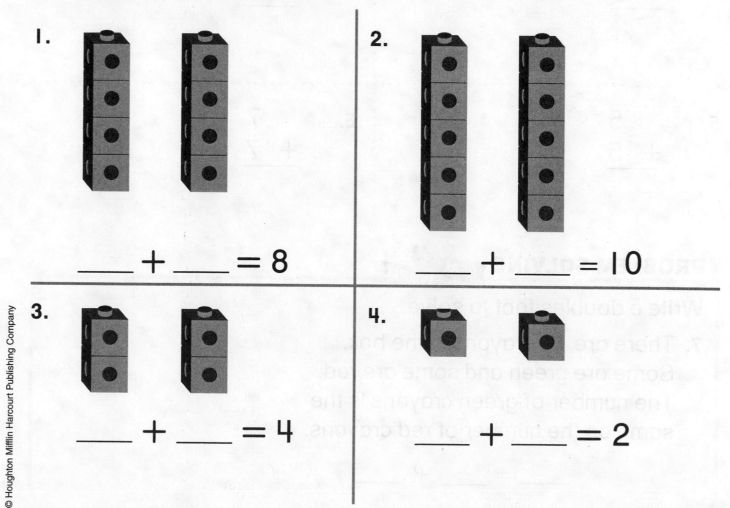

1.

____ + ____ = 8

2.

____ + ____ = 10

3.

____ + ____ = 4

4.

____ + ____ = 2

Name _____

Add Doubles

Use ⬛. Draw ⬛ to show your work.
Write the sum.

1.   4
    + 4

2.   6
    + 6

3.   3
    + 3

4.   8
    + 8

5.   5
    + 5

6.   7
    + 7

PROBLEM SOLVING   REAL WORLD

Write a doubles fact to solve.

7. There are 16 crayons in the box.
   Some are green and some are red.
   The number of green crayons is the
   same as the number of red crayons.

   ____ = ____ + ____

Use Doubles to Add

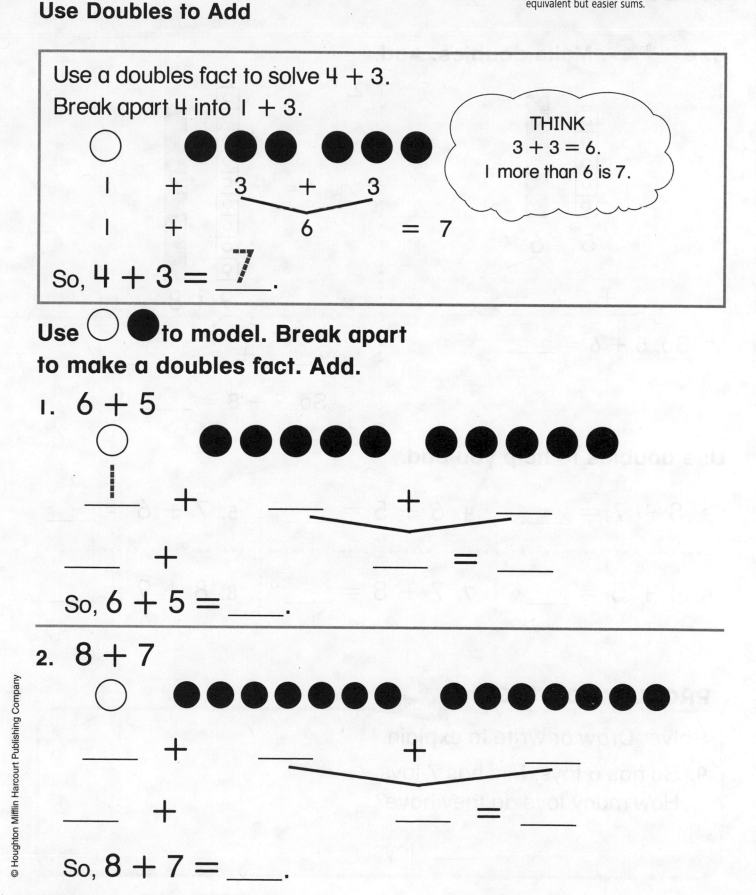

Use a doubles fact to solve 4 + 3.
Break apart 4 into 1 + 3.

○ ● ● ● ● ● ●

1 + 3 + 3

1 + 6 = 7

THINK
3 + 3 = 6.
1 more than 6 is 7.

So, 4 + 3 = **7**.

Use ○ ● to model. Break apart
to make a doubles fact. Add.

1. 6 + 5

○ ● ● ● ● ● ● ● ● ● ●

___ + ___ + ___

___ + ___ = ___

So, 6 + 5 = ___.

2. 8 + 7

○ ● ● ● ● ● ● ● ● ● ● ● ● ● ●

___ + ___ + ___

___ + ___ = ___

So, 8 + 7 = ___.

Operations and Algebraic Thinking

Name _____

Use Doubles to Add

Use 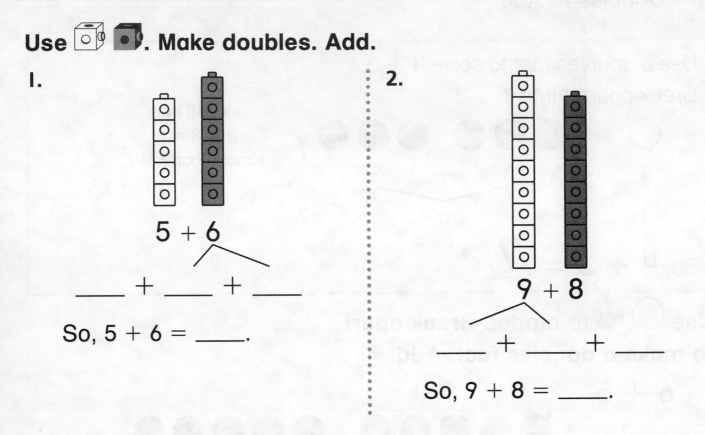 . Make doubles. Add.

1.

5 + 6

___ + ___ + ___

So, 5 + 6 = ___.

2.

9 + 8

___ + ___ + ___

So, 9 + 8 = ___.

Use doubles to help you add.

3. 8 + 7 = ___

4. 6 + 5 = ___

5. 7 + 6 = ___

6. 4 + 5 = ___

7. 7 + 8 = ___

8. 8 + 9 = ___

PROBLEM SOLVING REAL WORLD

Solve. Draw or write to explain.

9. Bo has 6 toys. Mia has 7 toys. How many toys do they have?

___ toys

Name _____

Lesson 29

COMMON CORE STANDARD CC.1.OA.6

Lesson Objective: Use doubles plus 1 and doubles minus 1 as strategies to find sums within 20.

Doubles Plus 1 and

Doubles Minus 1

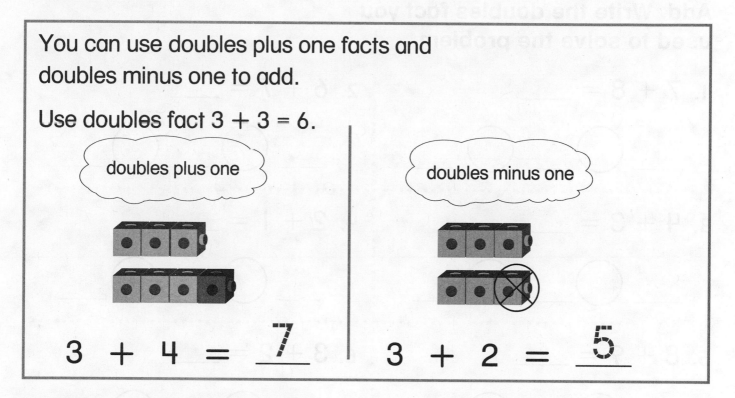

You can use doubles plus one facts and doubles minus one to add.

Use doubles fact 3 + 3 = 6.

doubles plus one

doubles minus one

3 + 4 = 7

3 + 2 = 5

Use doubles plus one or

doubles minus one to add.

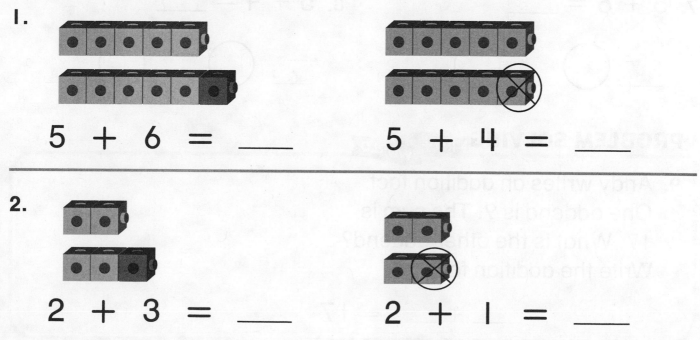

1.

5 + 6 = ___

5 + 4 = ___

2.

2 + 3 = ___

2 + 1 = ___

Operations and Algebraic Thinking

Name _____

Doubles Plus 1 and Doubles Minus 1

**Add. Write the doubles fact you
used to solve the problem.**

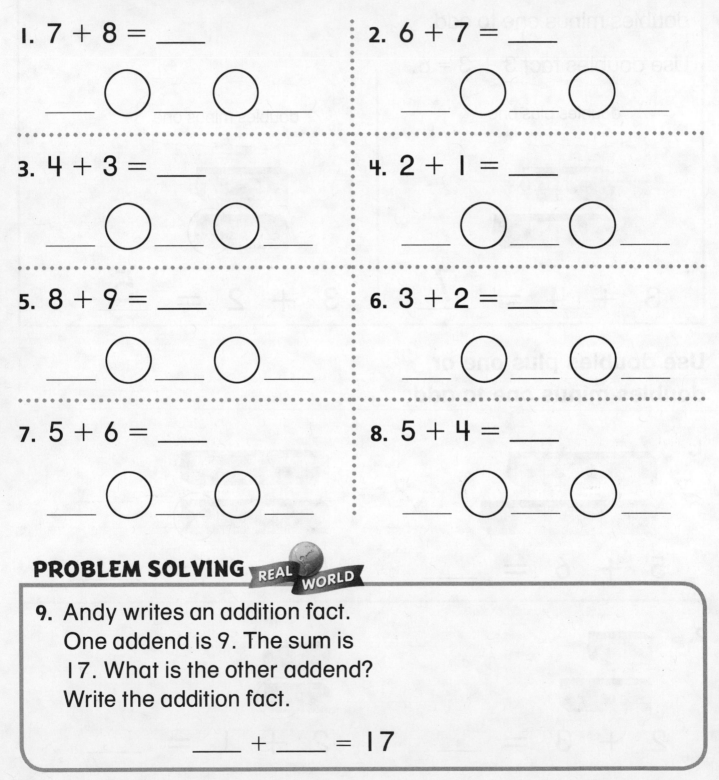

1. 7 + 8 = _____

___ ⃝ ___ ⃝ ___

2. 6 + 7 = _____

___ ⃝ ___ ⃝ ___

3. 4 + 3 = _____

___ ⃝ ___ ⃝ ___

4. 2 + 1 = _____

___ ⃝ ___ ⃝ ___

5. 8 + 9 = _____

___ ⃝ ___ ⃝ ___

6. 3 + 2 = _____

___ ⃝ ___ ⃝ ___

7. 5 + 6 = _____

___ ⃝ ___ ⃝ ___

8. 5 + 4 = _____

___ ⃝ ___ ⃝ ___

PROBLEM SOLVING REAL WORLD

9. Andy writes an addition fact.
One addend is 9. The sum is
17. What is the other addend?
Write the addition fact.

_____ + _____ = 17

Name _____

Lesson 30

COMMON CORE STANDARD CC.1.OA.6
Lesson Objective: Use the strategies count on, doubles, doubles plus 1, and doubles minus 1 to practice addition facts within 20.

Practice the Strategies

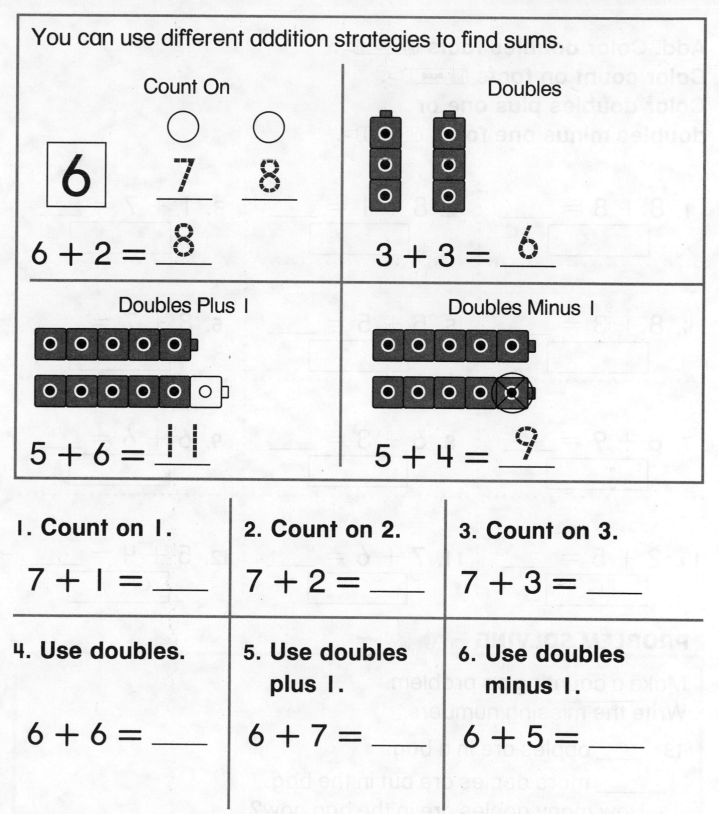

You can use different addition strategies to find sums.

Count On

6   7   8

6 + 2 = 8

Doubles

3 + 3 = 6

Doubles Plus 1

5 + 6 = 11

Doubles Minus 1

5 + 4 = 9

1. Count on 1.

7 + 1 = ___

2. Count on 2.

7 + 2 = ___

3. Count on 3.

7 + 3 = ___

4. Use doubles.

6 + 6 = ___

5. Use doubles plus 1.

6 + 7 = ___

6. Use doubles minus 1.

6 + 5 = ___

Operations and Algebraic Thinking

Name _____

Practice the Strategies

Add. Color doubles facts 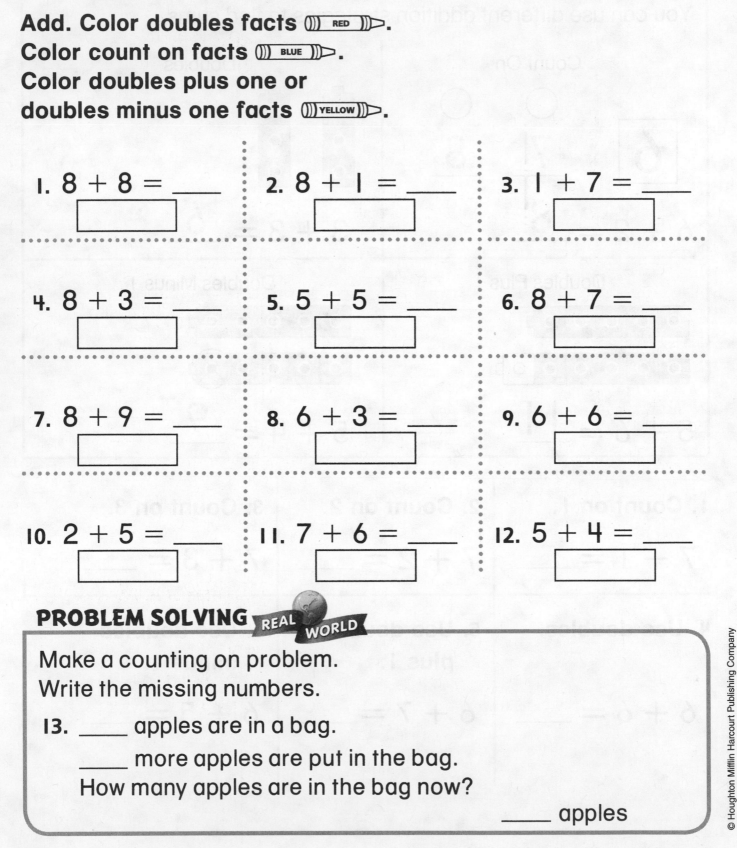 RED.
Color count on facts BLUE.
Color doubles plus one or
doubles minus one facts YELLOW.

1. $8 + 8 =$ ___

2. $8 + 1 =$ ___

3. $1 + 7 =$ ___

4. $8 + 3 =$ ___

5. $5 + 5 =$ ___

6. $8 + 7 =$ ___

7. $8 + 9 =$ ___

8. $6 + 3 =$ ___

9. $6 + 6 =$ ___

10. $2 + 5 =$ ___

11. $7 + 6 =$ ___

12. $5 + 4 =$ ___

PROBLEM SOLVING REAL WORLD

Make a counting on problem.
Write the missing numbers.

13. ____ apples are in a bag.

   ____ more apples are put in the bag.
   How many apples are in the bag now?

   ____ apples

Add 10 and More

You can use counters and a ten frame to add a number to 10.

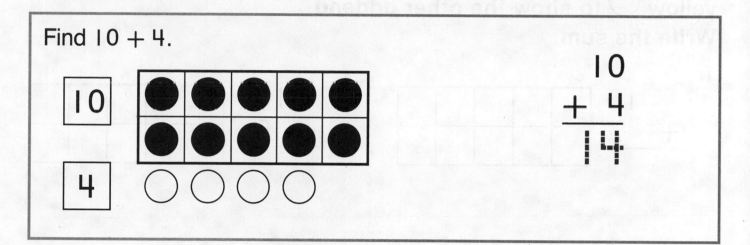

Draw ◯. Show the number that is added to 10.
Write the sum.

1.

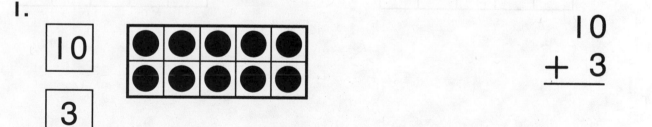

2.

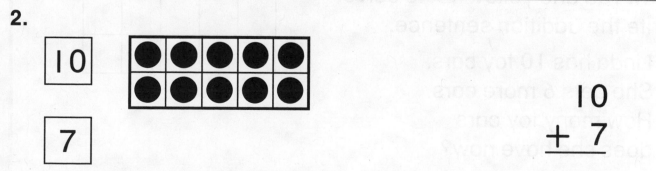

Add 10 and More

Draw red ◯ to show 10. Draw
yellow ◯ to show the other addend.
Write the sum.

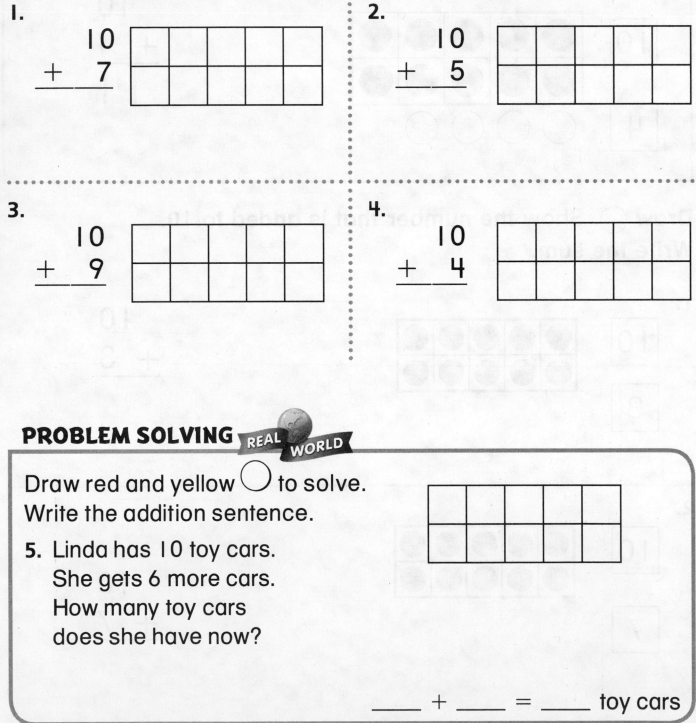

1. 10
    + 7
    _____

2. 10
    + 5
    _____

3. 10
    + 9
    _____

4. 10
    + 4
    _____

PROBLEM SOLVING REAL WORLD

Draw red and yellow ◯ to solve.
Write the addition sentence.

5. Linda has 10 toy cars.
   She gets 6 more cars.
   How many toy cars
   does she have now?

_____ + _____ = _____ toy cars

Lesson 32
COMMON CORE STANDARD CC.1.OA.6

Lesson Objective: Use make a ten as a strategy to find sums within 20.

Make a 10 to Add

Show 8 + 5 with counters and a ten frame.

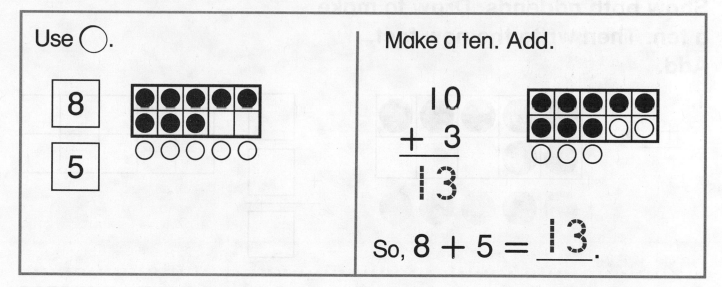

Use ◯.

| 8 |
| 5 |

Make a ten. Add.

10
+ 3
13

So, 8 + 5 = 13.

Draw ◯ to show the second addend. Make a ten. Add.

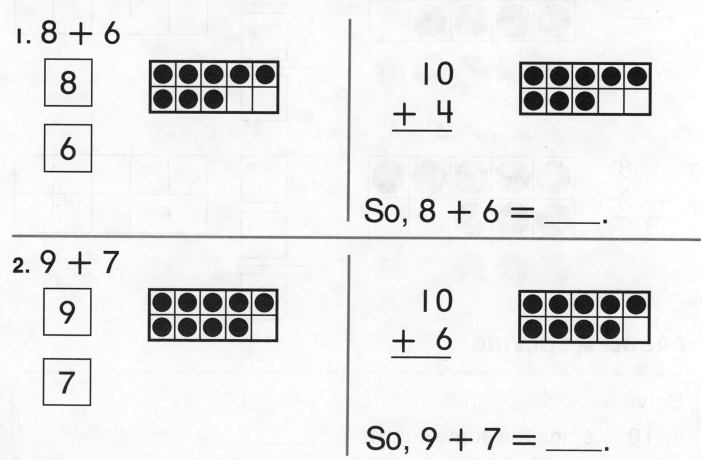

1. 8 + 6

| 8 |
| 6 |

10
+ 4

So, 8 + 6 = ___.

2. 9 + 7

| 9 |
| 7 |

10
+ 6

So, 9 + 7 = ___.

Operations and Algebraic Thinking

Make a 10 to Add

Use red and yellow ◯ and a ten frame.
Show both addends. Draw to make
a ten. Then write the new fact.
Add.

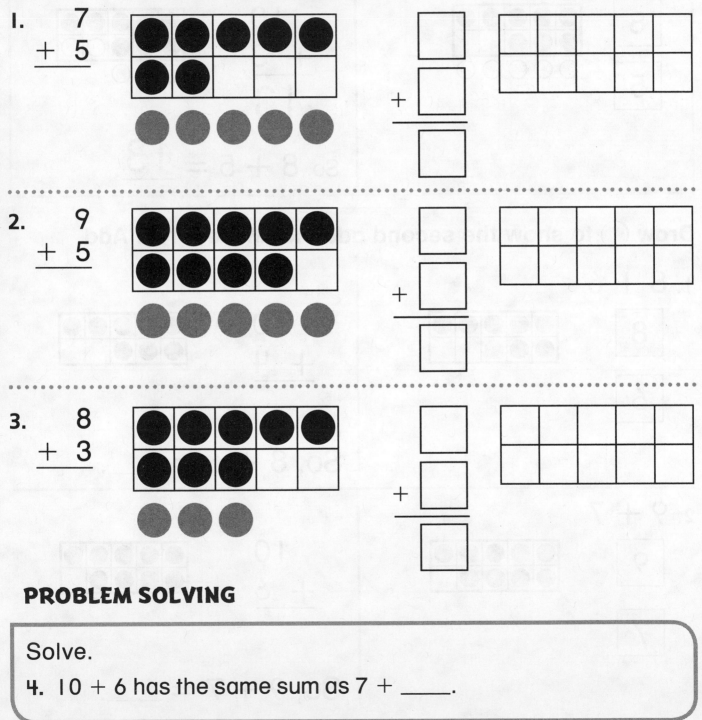

1. 7
  + 5

2. 9
  + 5

3. 8
  + 3

PROBLEM SOLVING

Solve.

4. 10 + 6 has the same sum as 7 + _____.

Name _____

Lesson 33
COMMON CORE STANDARD CC.1.OA.6
Lesson Objective: Use numbers to show how to use the make a ten strategy to add.

Use Make a 10 to Add

What is 9 + 5? Make a 10 to add.

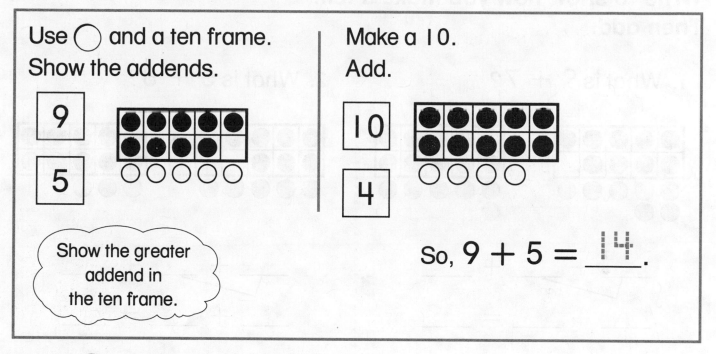

Use ◯ and a ten frame.
Show the addends.

9

5

Show the greater addend in the ten frame.

Make a 10.
Add.

10

4

So, 9 + 5 = __14__.

Draw ◯. Make a ten to add.

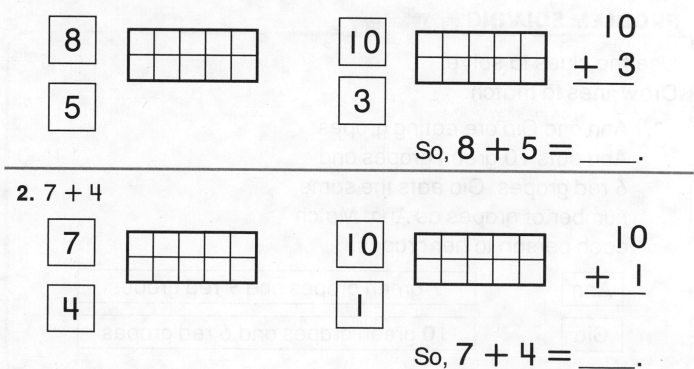

1. 8 + 5

8

5

10

3

10
+ 3

So, 8 + 5 = ___.

2. 7 + 4

7

4

10

1

10
+ 1

So, 7 + 4 = ___.

Operations and Algebraic Thinking

Name _____

Use Make a 10 to Add

**Write to show how you make a ten.
Then add.**

1. What is 9 + 7?

___ + ___ + ___

___ + ___ = ___

So, 9 + 7 = ____.

2. What is 5 + 8?

___ + ___ + ___

___ + ___ = ___

So, 5 + 8 = ____.

PROBLEM SOLVING   REAL WORLD

Use the clues to solve.
Draw lines to match.

3. Ann and Gia are eating grapes.
Ann eats 10 green grapes and
6 red grapes. Gia eats the same
number of grapes as Ann. Match
each person to her grapes.

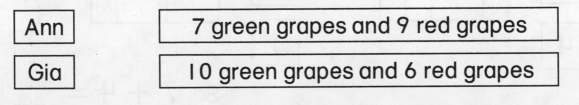

| Ann | | 7 green grapes and 9 red grapes |
| Gia | | 10 green grapes and 6 red grapes |

Lesson 34

COMMON CORE STANDARD CC.1.OA.6

Lesson Objective: Use make a 10 as a strategy to subtract.

Use 10 to Subtract

Find 14 – 9.

Start with 9 cubes.

Make a 10.

Add cubes to make 14.

Count what you added.

You added ___5___.

So, 14 – 9 = ___5___.

Use ⬛. **Make a ten to subtract.**
Draw to show your work.

1. 12 – 8 = __?__

   12 – 8 = ___

2. 15 – 9 = __?__

   15 – 9 = ___

Use 10 to Subtract

Use 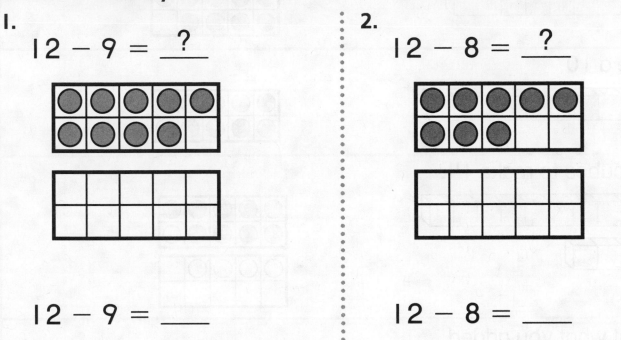 and ten frames. Make a
ten to subtract.
Draw to show your work.

1.
$$12 - 9 = \underline{}$$

$$12 - 9 = \underline{}$$

2.
$$12 - 8 = \underline{}$$

$$12 - 8 = \underline{}$$

PROBLEM SOLVING REAL WORLD

Solve. Use the ten frames to
make a ten to help you subtract.

3. Marta has 15 stickers.
8 are blue and the rest are red.
How many stickers are red?

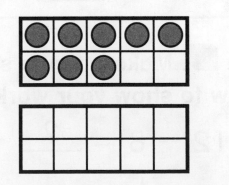

_____ stickers

Name _____

Lesson 35
COMMON CORE STANDARD CC.1.OA.6
Lesson Objective: Subtract by breaking apart to make a ten.

Break Apart to Subtract

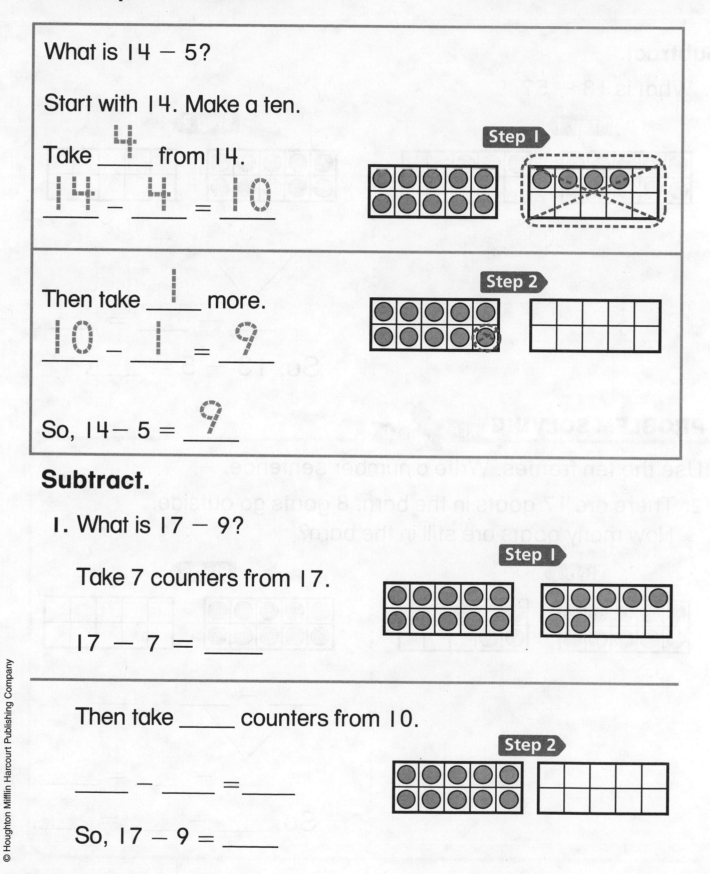

What is 14 − 5?

Start with 14. Make a ten.

Take __4__ from 14.

14 − 4 = 10

Step 1

Then take __1__ more.

10 − 1 = 9

Step 2

So, 14 − 5 = __9__

Subtract.

1. What is 17 − 9?

   Take 7 counters from 17.

   17 − 7 = ____

   Step 1

   Then take ____ counters from 10.

   ____ − ____ = ____

   Step 2

   So, 17 − 9 = ____

Operations and Algebraic Thinking

Break Apart to Subtract

Subtract.

1. What is 13 − 5?

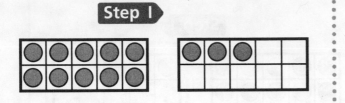

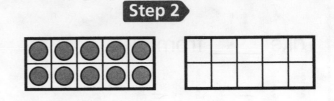

So, 13 − 5 = ___.

PROBLEM SOLVING REAL WORLD

Use the ten frames. Write a number sentence.

2. There are 17 goats in the barn. 8 goats go outside.
How many goats are still in the barn?

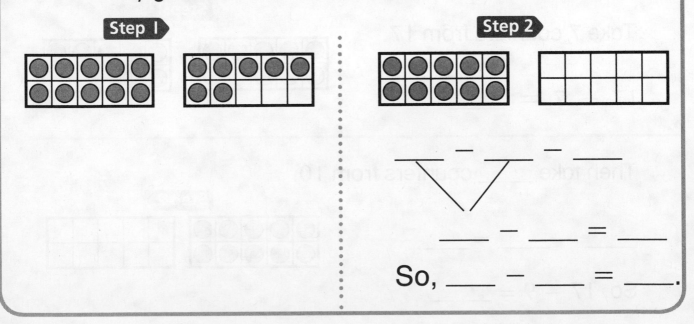

So, ___ − ___ = ___.

Record Related Facts

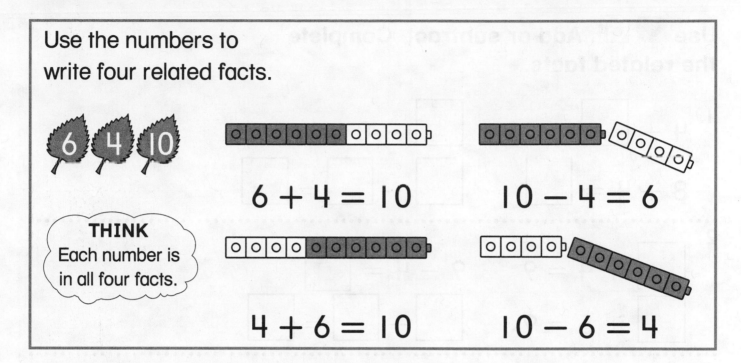

Use the numbers to write four related facts.

6 4 10

THINK
Each number is in all four facts.

$6 + 4 = 10$ $10 - 4 = 6$

$4 + 6 = 10$ $10 - 6 = 4$

Use the numbers to make related facts.

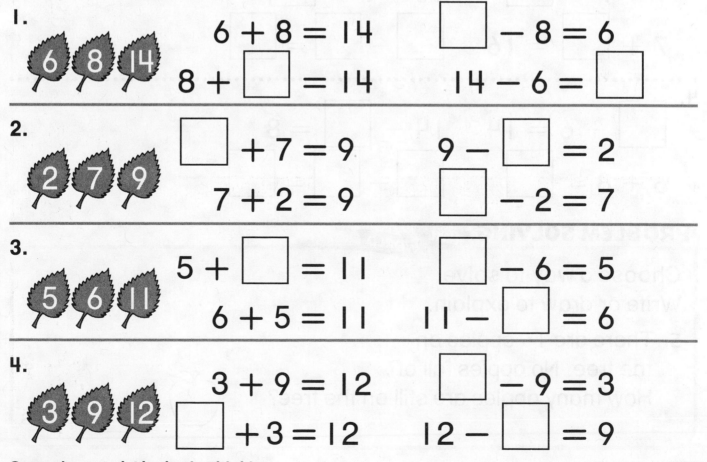

1. 6 8 14

$6 + 8 = 14$ $\square - 8 = 6$

$8 + \square = 14$ $14 - 6 = \square$

2. 2 7 9

$\square + 7 = 9$ $9 - \square = 2$

$7 + 2 = 9$ $\square - 2 = 7$

3. 5 6 11

$5 + \square = 11$ $\square - 6 = 5$

$6 + 5 = 11$ $11 - \square = 6$

4. 3 9 12

$3 + 9 = 12$ $\square - 9 = 3$

$\square + 3 = 12$ $12 - \square = 9$

Operations and Algebraic Thinking

Record Related Facts

Use 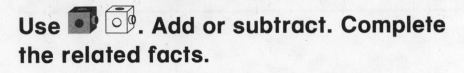. Add or subtract. Complete the related facts.

1.
$$4 + \boxed{} = 12 \qquad \boxed{} - 8 = 4$$

$$8 + 4 = \boxed{} \qquad \boxed{} - \boxed{} = \boxed{}$$

2.
$$\boxed{} + 4 = 9 \qquad 9 - 4 = \boxed{}$$

$$\boxed{} + 5 = 9 \qquad \boxed{} - \boxed{} = \boxed{}$$

3.
$$9 + 7 = \boxed{} \qquad 16 - 7 = \boxed{}$$

$$7 + \boxed{} = 16 \qquad \boxed{} - \boxed{} = \boxed{}$$

4.
$$\boxed{} + 6 = 14 \qquad 14 - \boxed{} = 8$$

$$6 + 8 = \boxed{} \qquad \boxed{} - \boxed{} = \boxed{}$$

PROBLEM SOLVING REAL WORLD

Choose a way to solve.
Write or draw to explain.

5. There are 16 apples on the tree. No apples fall off. How many apples are still on the tree?

_____ apples

Lesson **37**

COMMON CORE STANDARD CC.1.OA.6

Lesson Objective: Identify related addition and subtraction facts within 20.

Name _____

Identify Related Facts

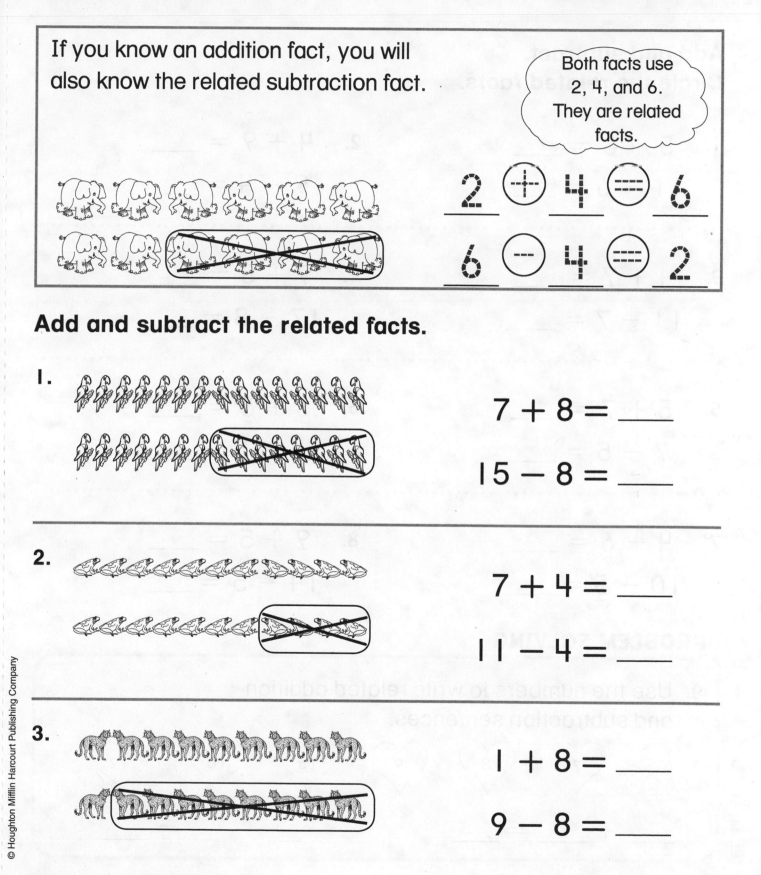

If you know an addition fact, you will also know the related subtraction fact.

Both facts use 2, 4, and 6. They are related facts.

$$2 + 4 = 6$$

$$6 - 4 = 2$$

Add and subtract the related facts.

1.

$$7 + 8 = \_\_\_$$

$$15 - 8 = \_\_\_$$

2.

$$7 + 4 = \_\_\_$$

$$11 - 4 = \_\_\_$$

3.

$$1 + 8 = \_\_\_$$

$$9 - 8 = \_\_\_$$

Operations and Algebraic Thinking

Identify Related Facts

Add and subtract.
Circle the related facts.

1. $5 + 6 =$ ___
   $11 - 6 =$ ___

2. $4 + 9 =$ ___
   $9 - 4 =$ ___

3. $4 + 7 =$ ___
   $11 - 7 =$ ___

4. $9 + 8 =$ ___
   $17 - 8 =$ ___

5. $5 + 7 =$ ___
   $7 - 5 =$ ___

6. $6 + 8 =$ ___
   $14 - 8 =$ ___

7. $4 + 6 =$ ___
   $10 - 5 =$ ___

8. $9 + 5 =$ ___
   $14 - 5 =$ ___

PROBLEM SOLVING

9. Use the numbers to write related addition and subtraction sentences.

6   7   8   9   15   16   17

___ + ___ = ___   ___ − ___ = ___

Name _____

Lesson 38

COMMON CORE STANDARD CC.1.OA.6

Lesson Objective: Apply the inverse relationship of addition and subtraction.

Use Addition to Check Subtraction

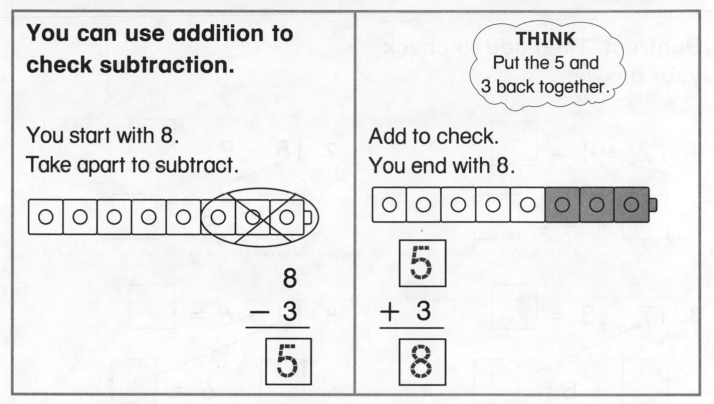

You can use addition to check subtraction.

You start with 8.
Take apart to subtract.

$$\begin{array}{r} 8 \\ -\ 3 \\ \hline \boxed{5} \end{array}$$

THINK
Put the 5 and 3 back together.

Add to check.
You end with 8.

$$\begin{array}{r} \boxed{5} \\ +\ 3 \\ \hline \boxed{8} \end{array}$$

Use 🎲 🎲 **to help you. Subtract.**
Then add to check your answer.

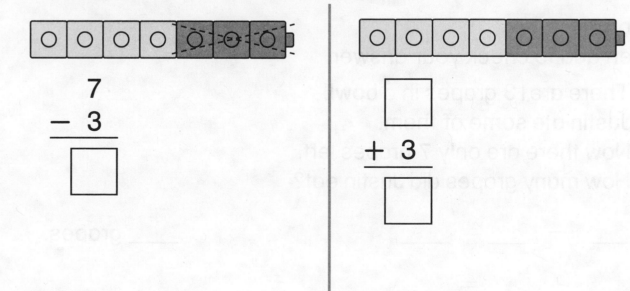

$$\begin{array}{r} 7 \\ -\ 3 \\ \hline \boxed{} \end{array}$$

$$\begin{array}{r} \boxed{} \\ +\ 3 \\ \hline \boxed{} \end{array}$$

Name _____

Use Addition to Check Subtraction

Subtract. Then add to check your answer.

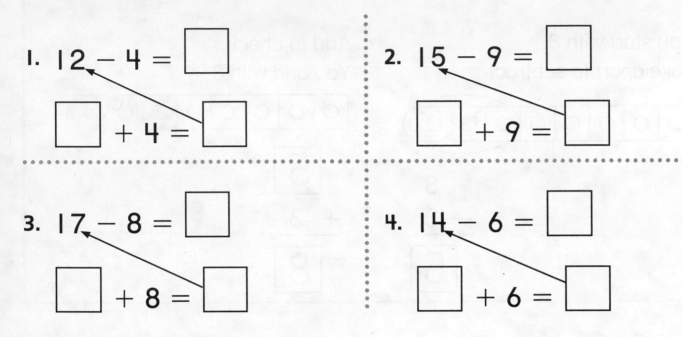

1. $12 - 4 = \boxed{}$

   $\boxed{} + 4 = \boxed{}$

2. $15 - 9 = \boxed{}$

   $\boxed{} + 9 = \boxed{}$

3. $17 - 8 = \boxed{}$

   $\boxed{} + 8 = \boxed{}$

4. $14 - 6 = \boxed{}$

   $\boxed{} + 6 = \boxed{}$

PROBLEM SOLVING REAL WORLD

Subtract.
Then add to check your answer.

5. There are 13 grapes in a bowl.
   Justin ate some of them.
   Now there are only 7 grapes left.
   How many grapes did Justin eat?

   ___ – ___ = ___   ___ grapes.

   ___ + ___ = ___

Algebra • Ways to Make Numbers to 20

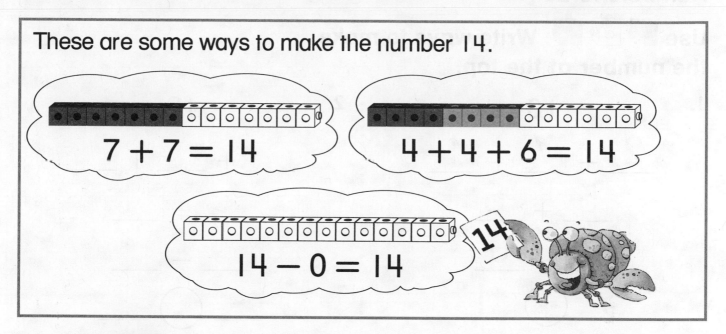

These are some ways to make the number 14.

$7 + 7 = 14$

$4 + 4 + 6 = 14$

$14 - 0 = 14$

Use ⚂ to show each way.

Cross out the way that does not make the number.

1. **7**	$8 - 1$	$3 + 4$	~~$2 + 3 + 1$~~
2. **15**	$7 + 6$	$15 - 0$	$8 + 7$
3. **13**	$4 + 4 + 5$	$9 - 4$	$6 + 7$
4. **9**	$8 + 2$	$3 + 3 + 3$	$10 - 1$
5. **18**	$9 + 9$	$9 - 9$	$18 - 0$

Algebra • Ways to Make Numbers to 20

Use 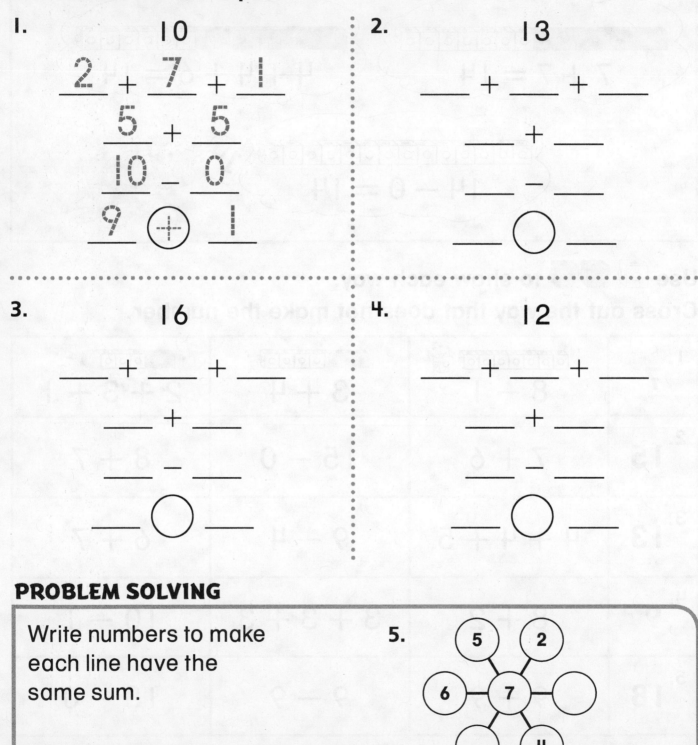. **Write ways to make the number at the top.**

1.
10

$2 + 7 + 1$

$5 + 5$

$10 - 0$

$9 \oplus 1$

2.
13

$\underline{} + \underline{} + \underline{}$

$\underline{} + \underline{}$

$\underline{} - \underline{}$

$\underline{} \bigcirc \underline{}$

3.
16

$\underline{} + \underline{} + \underline{}$

$\underline{} + \underline{}$

$\underline{} - \underline{}$

$\underline{} \bigcirc \underline{}$

4.
12

$\underline{} + \underline{} + \underline{}$

$\underline{} + \underline{}$

$\underline{} - \underline{}$

$\underline{} \bigcirc \underline{}$

PROBLEM SOLVING

Write numbers to make each line have the same sum.

5.

⑤ ②
⑥ ⑦ ◯
◯ ④

Lesson 40

COMMON CORE STANDARD CC.1.OA.6

Lesson Objective: Add and subtract facts within 20 and demonstrate fluency for addition and subtraction within 10.

Name _____

Basic Facts to 20

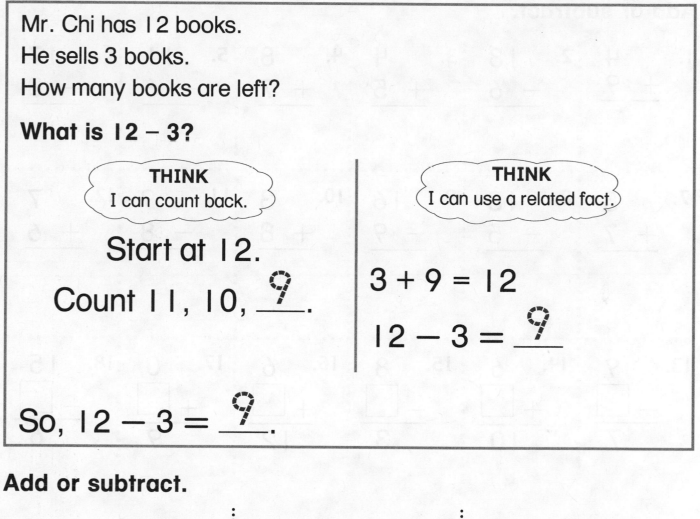

Mr. Chi has 12 books.

He sells 3 books.

How many books are left?

What is 12 − 3?

THINK
I can count back.

Start at 12.

Count 11, 10, __9__.

So, 12 − 3 = __9__.

THINK
I can use a related fact.

$3 + 9 = 12$

$12 − 3 = $ __9__

Add or subtract.

1. $14 − 5 = $ ___

2. $9 + 2 = $ ___

3. $6 + 4 = $ ___

4. $12 − 6 = $ ___

5. $8 − 3 = $ ___

6. $7 + 5 = $ ___

7. $9 + 6 = $ ___

8. $13 − 9 = $ ___

9. $8 + 8 = $ ___

Operations and Algebraic Thinking

Basic Facts to 20

Add or subtract.

1. $\begin{array}{r} 4 \\ + 9 \\ \hline \end{array}$

2. $\begin{array}{r} 13 \\ - 6 \\ \hline \end{array}$

3. $\begin{array}{r} 4 \\ + 5 \\ \hline \end{array}$

4. $\begin{array}{r} 8 \\ + 7 \\ \hline \end{array}$

5. $\begin{array}{r} 11 \\ - 6 \\ \hline \end{array}$

6. $\begin{array}{r} 17 \\ - 8 \\ \hline \end{array}$

7. $\begin{array}{r} 5 \\ + 7 \\ \hline \end{array}$

8. $\begin{array}{r} 13 \\ - 5 \\ \hline \end{array}$

9. $\begin{array}{r} 16 \\ - 9 \\ \hline \end{array}$

10. $\begin{array}{r} 3 \\ + 8 \\ \hline \end{array}$

11. $\begin{array}{r} 9 \\ - 8 \\ \hline \end{array}$

12. $\begin{array}{r} 7 \\ + 6 \\ \hline \end{array}$

13. $\begin{array}{r} 9 \\ - \square \\ \hline 7 \end{array}$

14. $\begin{array}{r} 6 \\ + \square \\ \hline 10 \end{array}$

15. $\begin{array}{r} 8 \\ - \square \\ \hline 3 \end{array}$

16. $\begin{array}{r} 6 \\ + \square \\ \hline 12 \end{array}$

17. $\begin{array}{r} 0 \\ + \square \\ \hline 9 \end{array}$

18. $\begin{array}{r} 15 \\ - \square \\ \hline 6 \end{array}$

PROBLEM SOLVING REAL WORLD

Solve. Draw or write to explain.

19. Kara has 9 drawings.
She gives 4 away. How many
drawings does Kara have now?

_____ drawings

Add and Subtract within 20

You can use strategies to add or subtract.

- count on
- doubles
- doubles plus one
- count back
- related facts
- doubles minus one

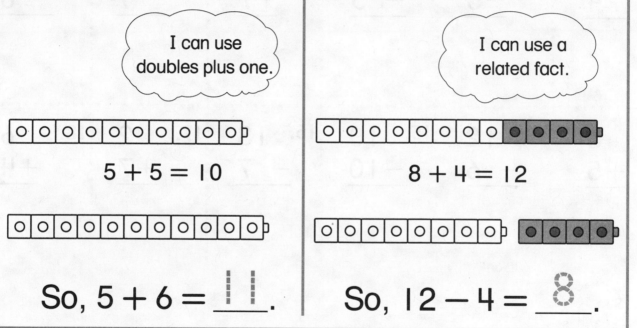

What is $5 + 6$?

I can use doubles plus one.

$5 + 5 = 10$

So, $5 + 6 = \underline{11}$.

What is $12 - 4$?

I can use a related fact.

$8 + 4 = 12$

So, $12 - 4 = \underline{8}$.

Add or subtract.

1. $12 - 3 = $ _____

2. $8 + 9 = $ _____

3. $10 - 5 = $ _____

4. $13 - 7 = $ _____

5. $7 + 8 = $ _____

6. $6 + 6 = $ _____

Add and Subtract within 20

Add or subtract.

1. $\begin{array}{r} 6 \\ +0 \\ \hline \end{array}$	2. $\begin{array}{r} 11 \\ -\ 2 \\ \hline \end{array}$	3. $\begin{array}{r} 4 \\ +5 \\ \hline \end{array}$	4. $\begin{array}{r} 9 \\ +8 \\ \hline \end{array}$	5. $\begin{array}{r} 4 \\ +10 \\ \hline \end{array}$	6. $\begin{array}{r} 14 \\ -\ 9 \\ \hline \end{array}$
7. $\begin{array}{r} 7 \\ +4 \\ \hline \end{array}$	8. $\begin{array}{r} 8 \\ -5 \\ \hline \end{array}$	9. $\begin{array}{r} 12 \\ -\ 3 \\ \hline \end{array}$	10. $\begin{array}{r} 6 \\ +7 \\ \hline \end{array}$	11. $\begin{array}{r} 18 \\ -\ 9 \\ \hline \end{array}$	12. $\begin{array}{r} 15 \\ -\ 6 \\ \hline \end{array}$
13. $\begin{array}{r} 6 \\ +5 \\ \hline \end{array}$	14. $\begin{array}{r} 12 \\ -\ 6 \\ \hline \end{array}$	15. $\begin{array}{r} 10 \\ -10 \\ \hline \end{array}$	16. $\begin{array}{r} 13 \\ -\ 7 \\ \hline \end{array}$	17. $\begin{array}{r} 2 \\ +7 \\ \hline \end{array}$	18. $\begin{array}{r} 6 \\ +4 \\ \hline \end{array}$

PROBLEM SOLVING REAL WORLD

Solve. Draw or write to explain.

19. Jesse has 4 shells. He finds some more. Now he has 12 shells. How many more shells did Jesse find?

_____ more shells

Name _____

Lesson 42
COMMON CORE STANDARD CC.1.OA.7
Lesson Objective: Determine if an equation is true or false.

Algebra • Equal and Not Equal

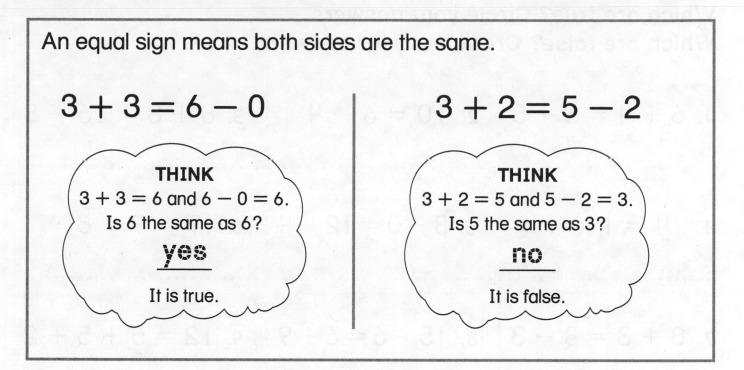

An equal sign means both sides are the same.

$$3 + 3 = 6 - 0$$

THINK
$3 + 3 = 6$ and $6 - 0 = 6$.
Is 6 the same as 6?

yes

It is true.

$$3 + 2 = 5 - 2$$

THINK
$3 + 2 = 5$ and $5 - 2 = 3$.
Is 5 the same as 3?

no

It is false.

Which is true? Circle your answer.
Which is false? Cross out your answer.

1. $7 - 5 = 5 - 2$

   $8 - 8 = 6 - 6$

2. $1 + 8 = 18$

   $2 + 8 = 8 + 2$

3. $4 + 3 = 5 + 2$

   $7 + 3 = 4 + 5$

4. $9 - 2 = 9 + 2$

   $9 = 10 - 1$

Operations and Algebraic Thinking

Algebra • Equal and Not Equal

Which are true? Circle your answers.
Which are false? Cross out your answers.

1. $6 + 4 = 5 + 5$

2. $10 = 6 - 4$

3. $8 + 8 = 16 - 8$

4. $14 = 1 + 4$

5. $8 - 0 = 12 - 4$

6. $17 = 9 + 8$

7. $8 + 3 = 8 - 3$

8. $15 - 6 = 6 + 9$

9. $12 = 5 + 5 + 2$

10. $7 + 6 = 6 + 7$

11. $5 - 4 = 4 + 5$

12. $0 + 9 = 9 - 0$

PROBLEM SOLVING REAL WORLD

13. Which are true? Use a ⬠⬠⬠ to color.

$15 = 15$	$12 = 2$	$3 = 8 - 5$
$15 = 1 + 5$	$9 + 2 = 2 + 9$	$9 + 2 = 14$
$1 + 2 + 3 = 3 + 3$	$5 - 3 = 5 + 3$	$13 = 8 + 5$

Use Pictures and Subtraction to Compare

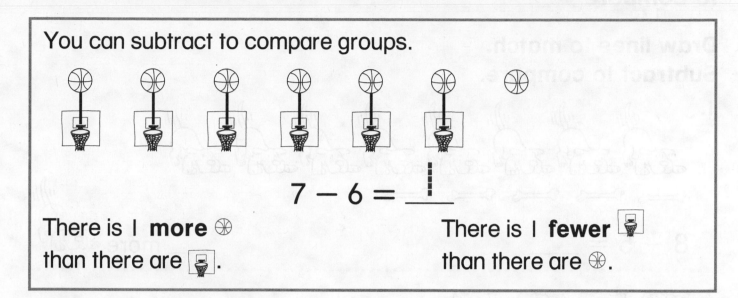

You can subtract to compare groups.

$7 - 6 = \underline{}$

There is 1 **more** ⊕ than there are 🏀.

There is 1 **fewer** 🏀 than there are ⊕.

Subtract to compare.

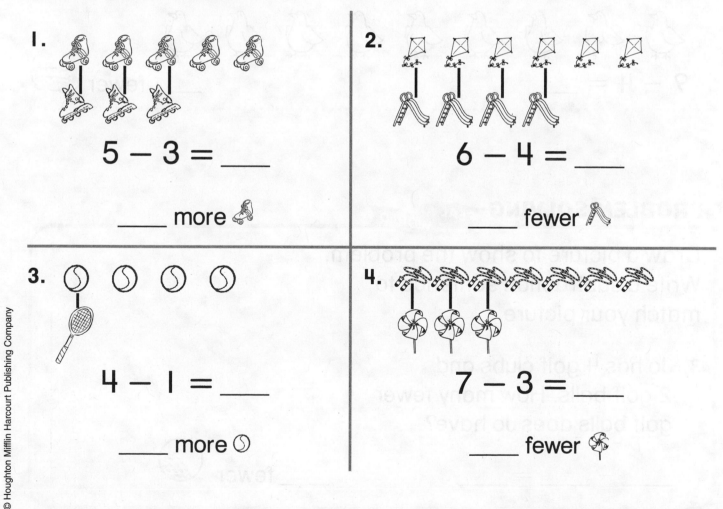

1. $5 - 3 = \underline{}$

_____ more 🛼

2. $6 - 4 = \underline{}$

_____ fewer 🪁

3. $4 - 1 = \underline{}$

_____ more ⚾

4. $7 - 3 = \underline{}$

_____ fewer 🎡

Use Pictures and Subtraction to Compare

Draw lines to match.
Subtract to compare.

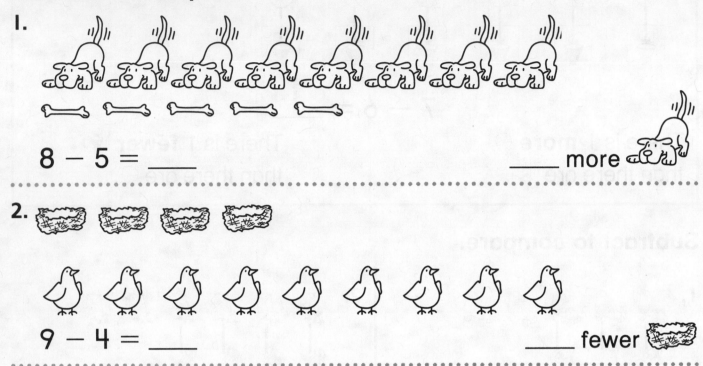

1. 8 − 5 = _____   _____ more

2. 9 − 4 = _____   _____ fewer

PROBLEM SOLVING REAL WORLD

Draw a picture to show the problem.
Write a subtraction sentence to
match your picture.

3. Jo has 4 golf clubs and
2 golf balls. How many fewer
golf balls does Jo have?

_____ − _____ = _____   _____ fewer

Name _____

Lesson 44
COMMON CORE STANDARD CC.1.OA.8
Lesson Objective: Identify how many are left when subtracting all or 0.

Subtract All or Zero

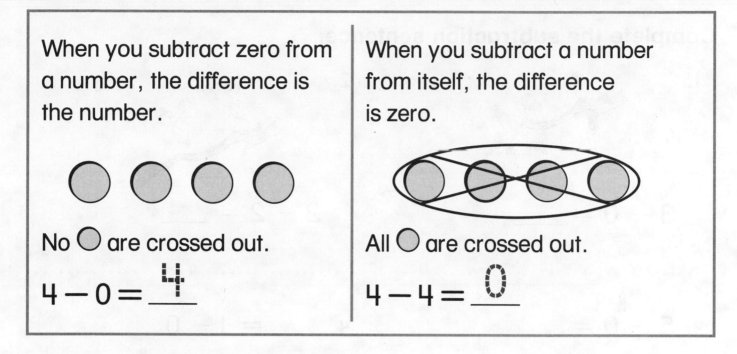

When you subtract zero from a number, the difference is the number.

No ◯ are crossed out.

$4 - 0 = \underline{4}$

When you subtract a number from itself, the difference is zero.

All ◯ are crossed out.

$4 - 4 = \underline{0}$

Use ◯. Write the difference.

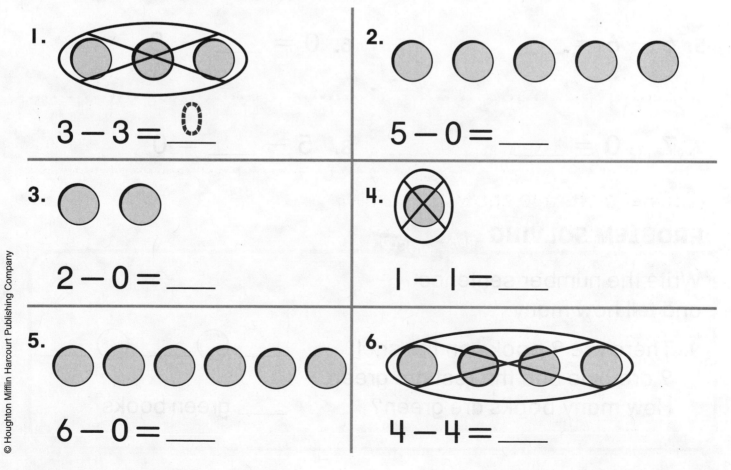

1.

$3 - 3 = \underline{0}$

2.

$5 - 0 = \underline{}$

3.

$2 - 0 = \underline{}$

4.

$1 - 1 = \underline{}$

5.

$6 - 0 = \underline{}$

6.

$4 - 4 = \underline{}$

Operations and Algebraic Thinking

Subtract All or Zero

Complete the subtraction sentence.

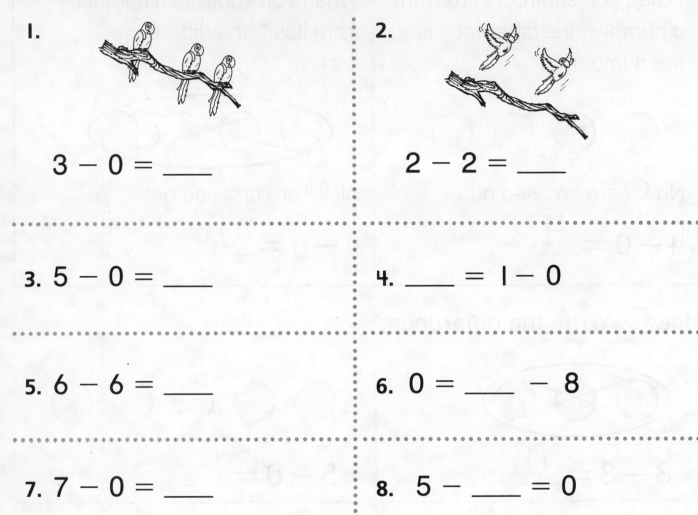

1.

$3 - 0 = $ ___

2.

$2 - 2 = $ ___

3. $5 - 0 = $ ___

4. ___ $= 1 - 0$

5. $6 - 6 = $ ___

6. $0 = $ ___ $- 8$

7. $7 - 0 = $ ___

8. $5 - $ ___ $= 0$

PROBLEM SOLVING REAL WORLD

Write the number sentence
and tell how many.

9. There are 9 books on the shelf.
   9 are blue and the rest are green.
   How many books are green?

___ ◯ ___ ◯ ___

___ green books

Name _____

Lesson 45
COMMON CORE STANDARD CC.1.OA.8
Lesson Objective: Use related facts to determine unknown numbers.

Algebra • Missing Numbers

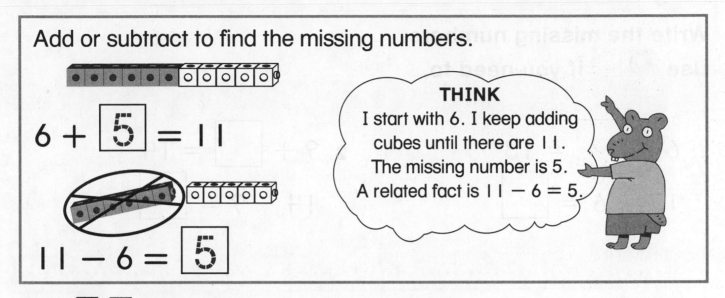

Add or subtract to find the missing numbers.

$6 + \boxed{5} = 11$

$11 - 6 = \boxed{5}$

THINK
I start with 6. I keep adding cubes until there are 11.
The missing number is 5.
A related fact is $11 - 6 = 5$.

Use 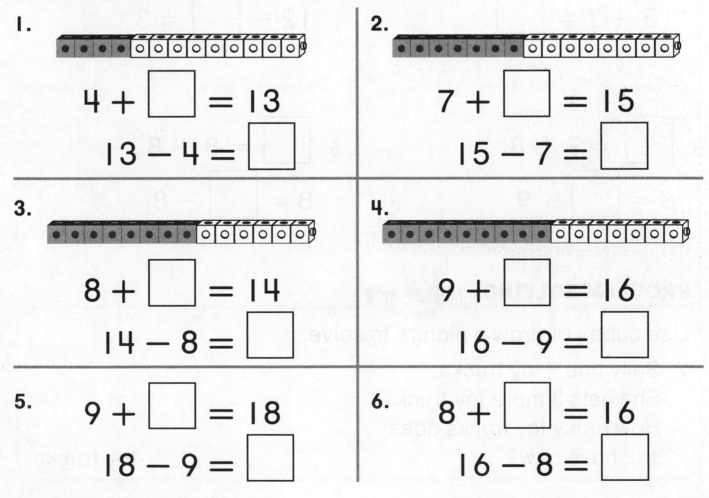 to find the missing numbers.
Write the numbers.

1.

$4 + \boxed{} = 13$

$13 - 4 = \boxed{}$

2.

$7 + \boxed{} = 15$

$15 - 7 = \boxed{}$

3.

$8 + \boxed{} = 14$

$14 - 8 = \boxed{}$

4.

$9 + \boxed{} = 16$

$16 - 9 = \boxed{}$

5.

$9 + \boxed{} = 18$

$18 - 9 = \boxed{}$

6.

$8 + \boxed{} = 16$

$16 - 8 = \boxed{}$

Operations and Algebraic Thinking

Algebra • Missing Numbers

Write the missing numbers.
Use 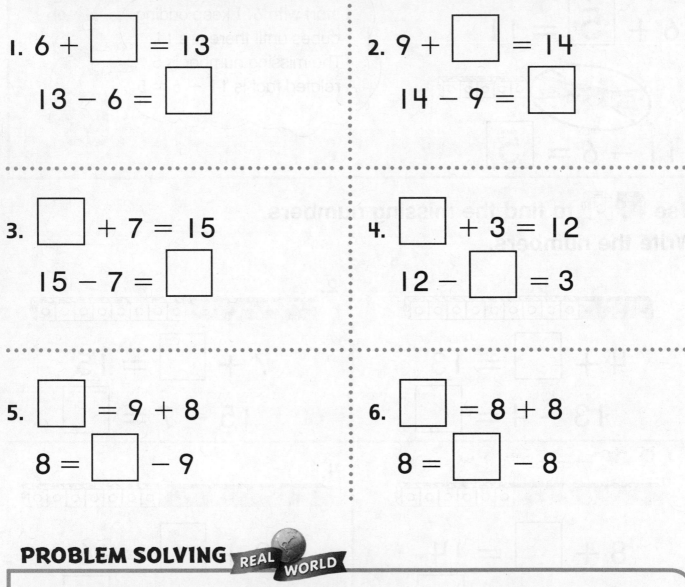 **if you need to.**

1. $6 + \boxed{} = 13$

   $13 - 6 = \boxed{}$

2. $9 + \boxed{} = 14$

   $14 - 9 = \boxed{}$

3. $\boxed{} + 7 = 15$

   $15 - 7 = \boxed{}$

4. $\boxed{} + 3 = 12$

   $12 - \boxed{} = 3$

5. $\boxed{} = 9 + 8$

   $8 = \boxed{} - 9$

6. $\boxed{} = 8 + 8$

   $8 = \boxed{} - 8$

PROBLEM SOLVING REAL WORLD

Use cubes or draw a picture to solve.

7. Sally has 9 toy trucks.
   She gets 3 more toy trucks.
   How many toy trucks does
   she have now?

   _____ toy trucks

Algebra • Use Related Facts

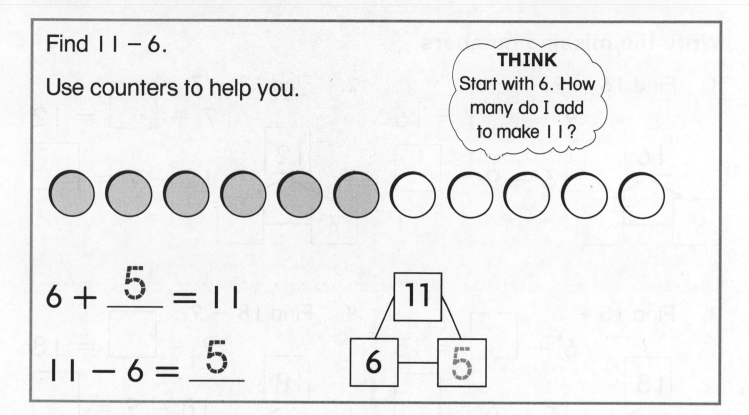

Find 11 − 6.

Use counters to help you.

THINK
Start with 6. How many do I add to make 11?

6 + __5__ = 11

11 − 6 = __5__

11
6   5

Use counters. Write the missing numbers.

1. Find 13 − 8.

8 + ___ = 13

13 − 8 = ___

13
8

2. Find 12 − 3.

3 + ___ = 12

12 − 3 = ___

12
3

Algebra • Use Related Facts

Write the missing numbers.

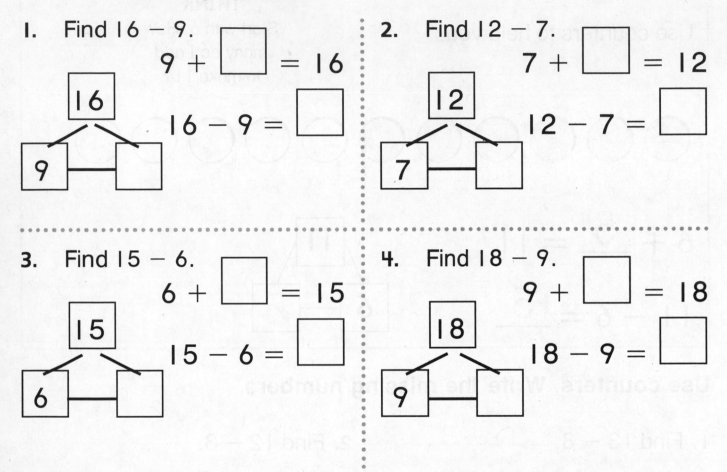

1.   Find 16 − 9.

9 + □ = 16

16 − 9 = □

2.   Find 12 − 7.

7 + □ = 12

12 − 7 = □

3.   Find 15 − 6.

6 + □ = 15

15 − 6 = □

4.   Find 18 − 9.

9 + □ = 18

18 − 9 = □

PROBLEM SOLVING

Look at the shapes in the addition sentence.
Draw a shape to show a related subtraction fact.

5.

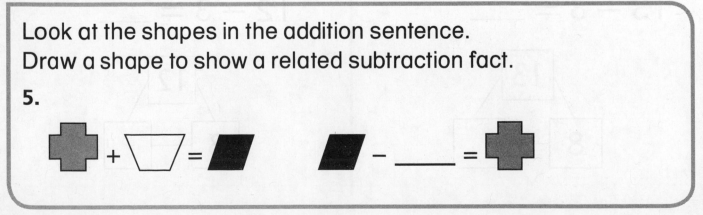

Name _____

Lesson 47

COMMON CORE STANDARD CC.1.NBT.1

Lesson Objective: Count by ones to extend a counting sequence up to 120.

Count by Ones to 120

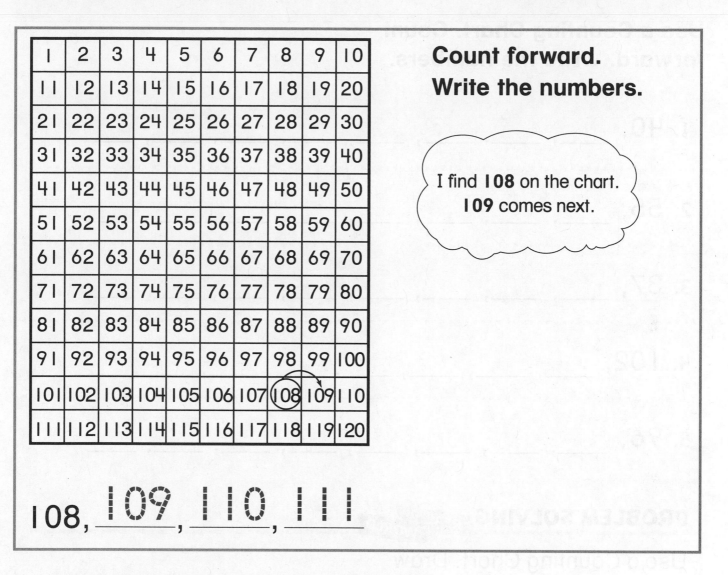

Count forward.
Write the numbers.

I find **108** on the chart.
109 comes next.

108, 109, 110, 111

Use a Counting Chart. Count forward.
Write the numbers.

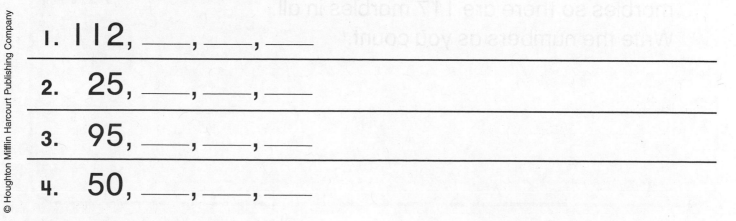

1. 112, ____, ____, ____

2. 25, ____, ____, ____

3. 95, ____, ____, ____

4. 50, ____, ____, ____

Number and Operations in Base Ten

Count by Ones to 120

Use a Counting Chart. Count forward. Write the numbers.

1. 40, ____, ____, ____, ____, ____, ____, ____, ____

2. 55, ____, ____, ____, ____, ____, ____, ____, ____, ____

3. 37, ____, ____, ____, ____, ____, ____, ____, ____

4. 102, ____, ____, ____, ____, ____, ____, ____, ____

5. 96, ____, ____, ____, ____, ____, ____, ____, ____

PROBLEM SOLVING REAL WORLD

Use a Counting Chart. Draw and write numbers to solve.

6. The bag has 111 marbles. Draw more marbles so there are 117 marbles in all. Write the numbers as you count.

111

Name _____

Lesson 48

COMMON CORE STANDARD CC.1.NBT.1

Lesson Objective: Count by tens from any number to extend a counting sequence up to 120.

Count by Tens to 120

Use the Counting Chart.
Count forward by tens.
Start on 4.

14, 24, 34, 44, 54,

64, 74, 84, 94,

104, 114

1	2	3	4	5	6	7	8	9	10
11	12	13	14	15	16	17	18	19	20
21	22	23	24	25	26	27	28	29	30
31	32	33	34	35	36	37	38	39	40
41	42	43	44	45	46	47	48	49	50
51	52	53	54	55	56	57	58	59	60
61	62	63	64	65	66	67	68	69	70
71	72	73	74	75	76	77	78	79	80
81	82	83	84	85	86	87	88	89	90
91	92	93	94	95	96	97	98	99	100
101	102	103	104	105	106	107	108	109	110
111	112	113	114	115	116	117	118	119	120

Use the Counting Chart to count by tens.
Write the numbers.

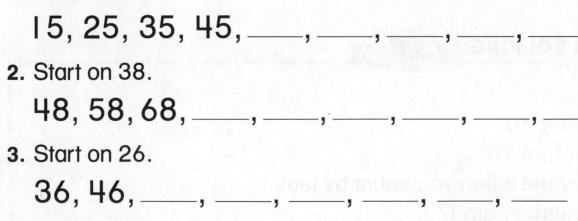

1. Start on 5.

15, 25, 35, 45, _____, _____, _____, _____, _____

2. Start on 38.

48, 58, 68, _____, _____, _____, _____, _____, _____

3. Start on 26.

36, 46, _____, _____, _____, _____, _____, _____

Count by Tens to 120

Use a Counting Chart.
Count by tens.
Write the numbers.

1. 1, ___, ___, ___, ___, ___, ___, ___, ___, ___

2. 14, ___, ___, ___, ___, ___, ___, ___, ___, ___

3. 7, ___, ___, ___, ___, ___, ___, ___, ___, ___

4. 29, ___, ___, ___, ___, ___, ___, ___, ___, ___

5. 5, ___, ___, ___, ___, ___, ___, ___, ___, ___

6. 12, ___, ___, ___, ___, ___, ___, ___, ___, ___

7. 26, ___, ___, ___, ___, ___, ___, ___, ___, ___

8. 3, ___, ___, ___, ___, ___, ___, ___, ___, ___

9. 8, ___, ___, ___, ___, ___, ___, ___, ___, ___

PROBLEM SOLVING REAL WORLD

Solve.

10. I am after 70.
I am before 90.
You say me when you count by tens.
What number am I? ___

Name _____

Lesson **49**

COMMON CORE STANDARD CC.1.NBT.1
Lesson Objective: Read and write numerals
to represent a number of 100 to 110 objects.

Model, Read, and Write
Numbers from 100 to 110

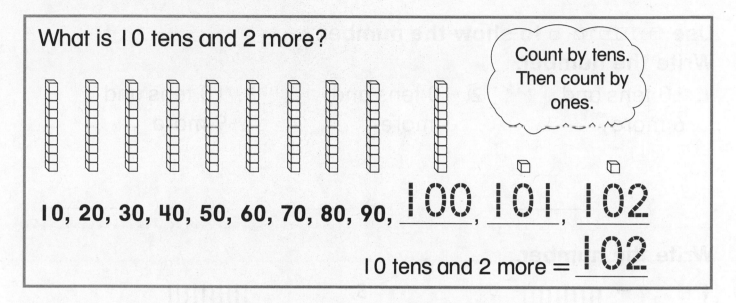

What is 10 tens and 2 more?

Count by tens.
Then count by ones.

10, 20, 30, 40, 50, 60, 70, 80, 90, **100**, **101**, **102**

10 tens and 2 more = **102**

Use ▱▱▱▱▱ ▱ to model the number.
Write the number.

1. 10 tens and 3 more

_____

2. 10 tens and 7 more

_____

3. 10 tens and 6 more

_____

4. 10 tens and 9 more

_____

Number and Operations in Base Ten

Model, Read, and Write Numbers from 100 to 110

Use 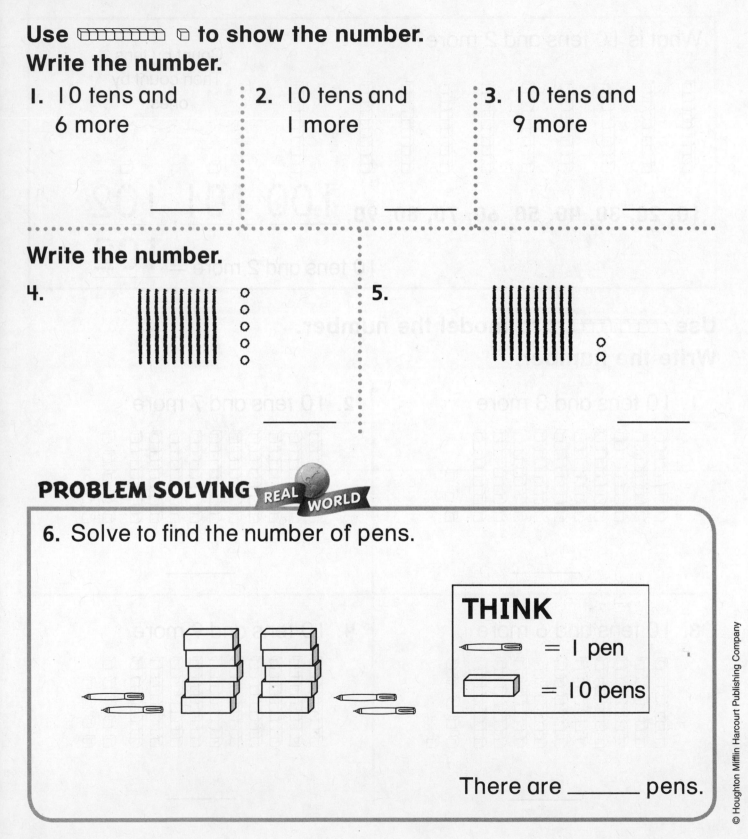 **to show the number.**
Write the number.

1. 10 tens and
6 more

_____

2. 10 tens and
1 more

_____

3. 10 tens and
9 more

_____

Write the number.

4.

|||||||||
  o
  o
  o
  o
  o

_____

5.

|||||||||
  o
  o

_____

PROBLEM SOLVING REAL WORLD

6. Solve to find the number of pens.

THINK

✒ = 1 pen

▭ = 10 pens

There are _____ pens.

Model, Read, and Write Numbers from 110 to 120

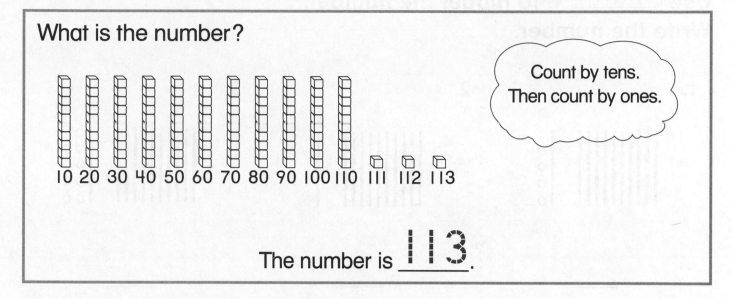

What is the number?

Count by tens.
Then count by ones.

10 20 30 40 50 60 70 80 90 100 110 111 112 113

The number is __113__.

Use ▭ ▱ to model the number.
Write the number.

1.

_____

2.

_____

3.

_____

4.

Model, Read, and Write
Numbers from 110 to 120

Use 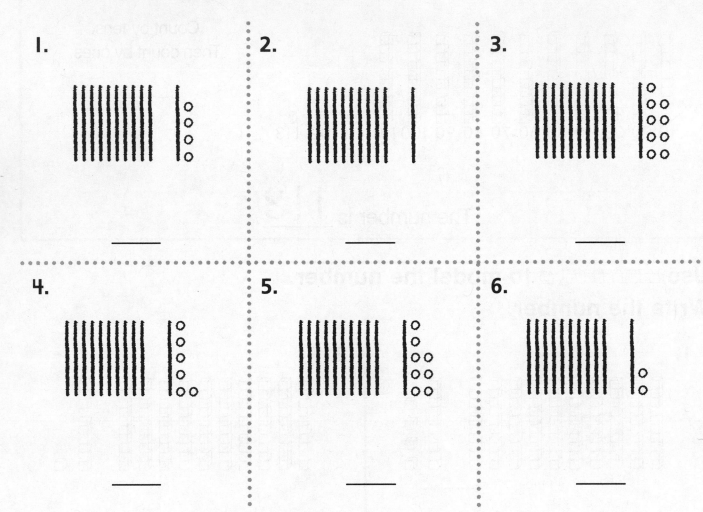 to model the number.
Write the number.

1. _____

2. _____

3. _____

4. _____

5. _____

6. _____

PROBLEM SOLVING REAL WORLD

Choose a way to solve. Draw or write to explain.

10. Dave collects rocks. He makes
12 groups of 10 rocks and has
none left over. How many rocks
does Dave have?   _____ rocks

Tens and Ones to 50

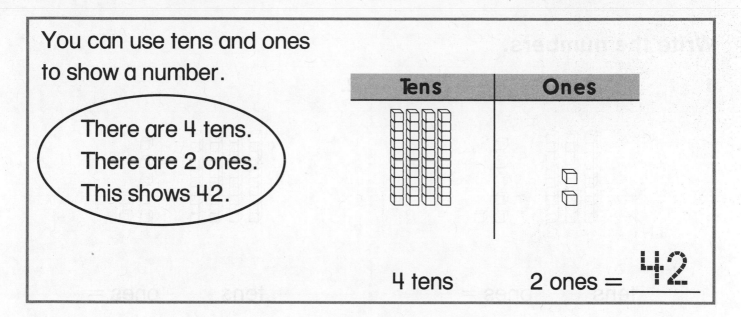

You can use tens and ones to show a number.

There are 4 tens.
There are 2 ones.
This shows 42.

Tens	Ones

4 tens   2 ones = __42__

Use ⬚⬚⬚⬚⬚⬚⬚⬚⬚⬚ ▫ to show the tens and ones.
Write the numbers.

I.

1 tens 8 ones = __18__

2.

2 tens 5 ones = _____

3.

4 tens 7 ones = _____

4.

3 tens 6 ones = _____

Tens and Ones to 50

Write the numbers.

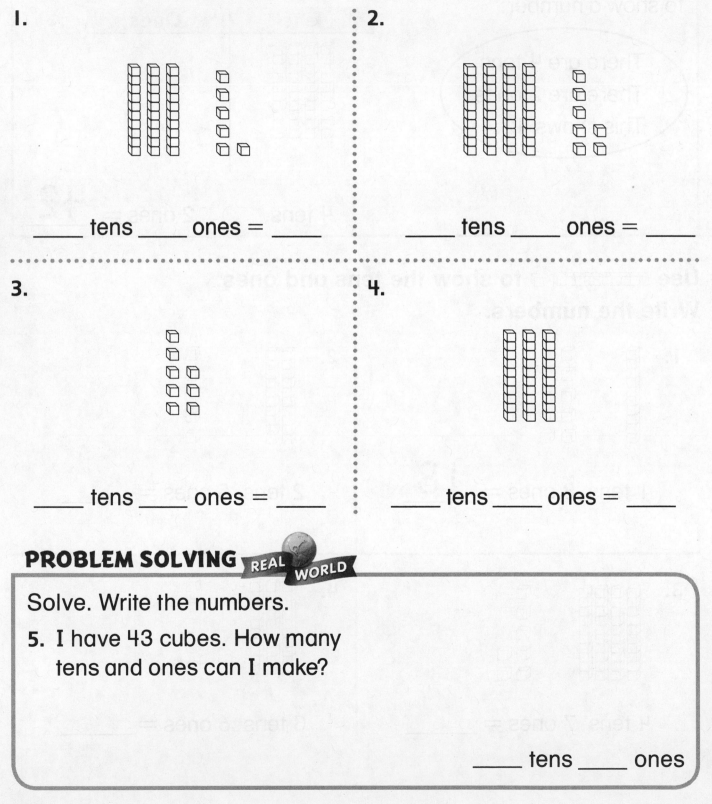

1.

____ tens ____ ones = ____

2.

____ tens ____ ones = ____

3.

____ tens ____ ones = ____

4.

____ tens ____ ones = ____

PROBLEM SOLVING REAL WORLD

Solve. Write the numbers.

5. I have 43 cubes. How many tens and ones can I make?

____ tens ____ ones

Tens and Ones to 100

If you know the tens and ones,
you can write the number.

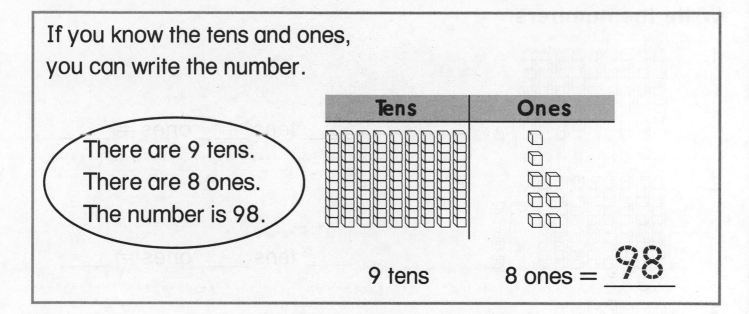

There are 9 tens.
There are 8 ones.
The number is 98.

Tens	Ones

9 tens   8 ones = 98

Use ⬚⬚⬚⬚ ⬚ **to show the tens and ones.**
Write the numbers.

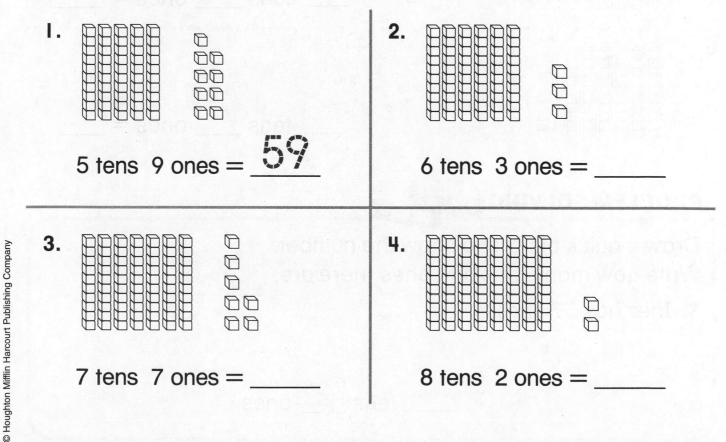

1. 5 tens 9 ones = 59

2. 6 tens 3 ones = _____

3. 7 tens 7 ones = _____

4. 8 tens 2 ones = _____

Tens and Ones to 100

Write the numbers.

1.

_____ tens _____ ones = _____

2.

_____ tens _____ ones = _____

3.

_____ tens _____ ones = _____

4.

_____ tens _____ ones = _____

PROBLEM SOLVING REAL WORLD

Draw a quick picture to show the number.
Write how many tens and ones there are.

5. Inez has 57 shells.

_____ tens _____ ones

Name _____

Lesson 53
COMMON CORE STANDARD CC.1.NBT.2a
Lesson Objective: Solve problems using the
strategy *make a model.*

Problem Solving • Show Numbers in Different Ways

How can you show the number 34 two different ways?

Unlock the Problem

What do I need to find?	**What information do I need to use?**
two different ways to show a number	The number is **34**.

Show how to solve the problem.

> **THINK**
> You can trade 1 ten for 10 ones.

First Way

Tens	Ones

Second Way

Tens	Ones

1. Use ▭▭▭▭▭▭▭ ▱ to show 26 two different ways. Draw both ways.

Tens	Ones

Tens	Ones

Problem Solving • Show Numbers in Different Ways

Use 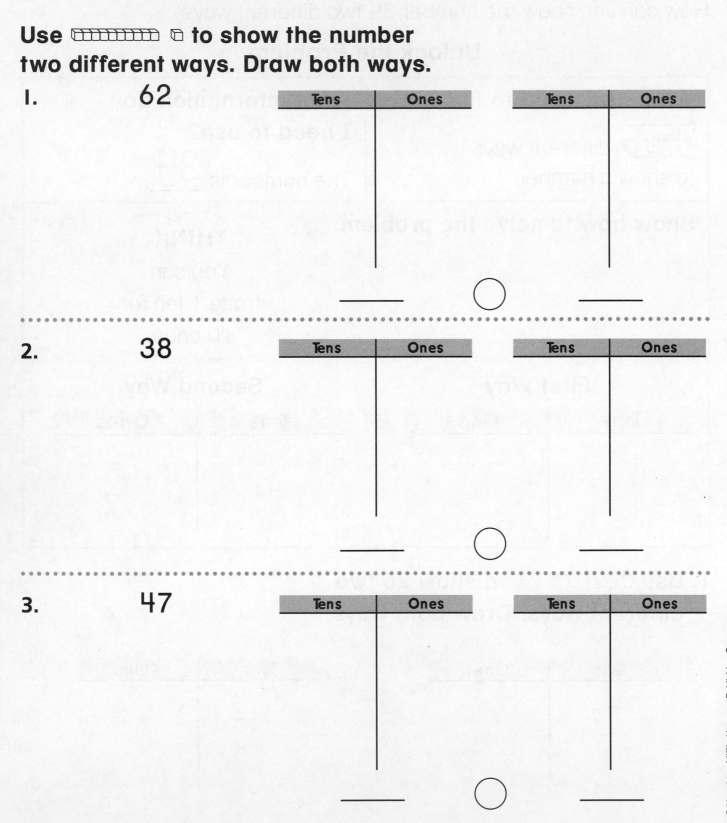 to show the number
two different ways. Draw both ways.

1. 62

Tens	Ones

Tens	Ones

    ____ ◯ ____

2. 38

Tens	Ones

Tens	Ones

    ____ ◯ ____

3. 47

Tens	Ones

Tens	Ones

    ____ ◯ ____

Lesson 54
COMMON CORE STANDARD CC.1.NBT.2b
Lesson Objective: Use models and write to
represent equivalent forms of ten and ones.

Understand Ten and Ones

You can use ⬚ to show ten and some ones.
You can write ten and ones in different ways.

$\underline{1}$ ten $\underline{2}$ ones

$\underline{10} + \underline{2}$

$\underline{12}$

Use the model. Write the number three different ways.

1.

_____ ten _____ ones

_____ + _____

_____

2.

_____ ten _____ ones

_____ + _____

_____

3.

_____ ten _____ ones

_____ + _____

_____

Understand Ten and Ones

**Use the model. Write the number
three different ways.**

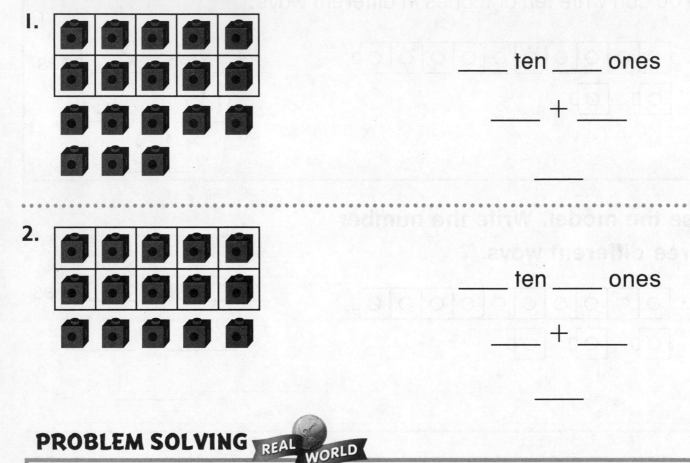

1.

___ ten ___ ones

___ + ___

___

2.

___ ten ___ ones

___ + ___

___

PROBLEM SOLVING REAL WORLD

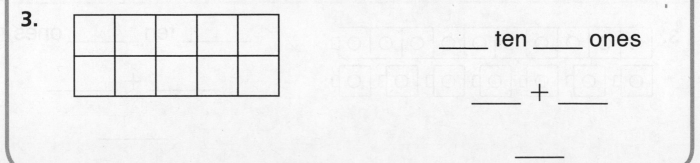

Draw cubes to show the number.
Write the number different ways.

Rob has 7 ones. Nick has 5 ones. They put all their
ones together. What number did they make?

3.

___ ten ___ ones

___ + ___

___

Make Ten and Ones

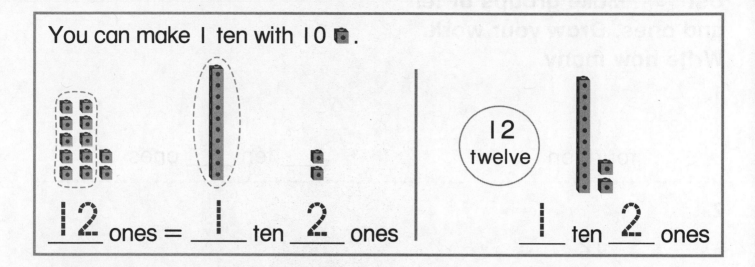

You can make 1 ten with 10 🔲.

12 ones = 1 ten 2 ones

12 twelve

1 ten 2 ones

Write how many tens and ones.

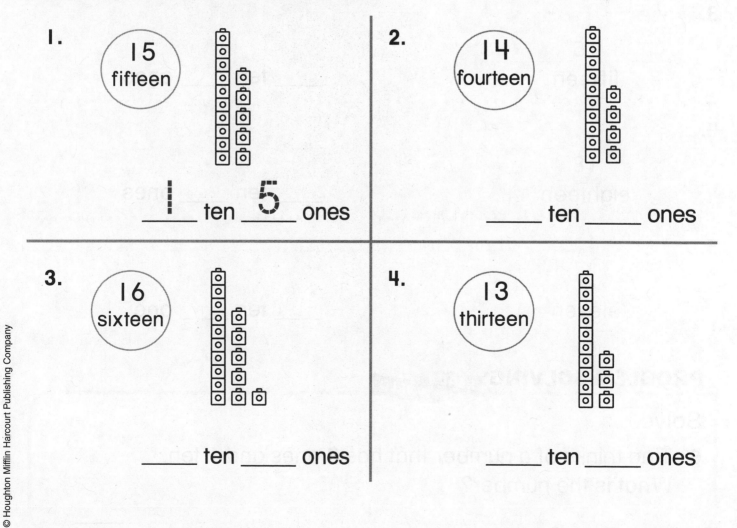

1. 15 fifteen

1 ten 5 ones

2. 14 fourteen

____ ten ____ ones

3. 16 sixteen

____ ten ____ ones

4. 13 thirteen

____ ten ____ ones

Make Ten and Ones

Use ⬚. Make groups of ten
and ones. Draw your work.
Write how many.

1.

14
fourteen

_____ ten _____ ones

2.

12
twelve

_____ ten _____ ones

3.

15
fifteen

_____ ten _____ ones

4.

18
eighteen

_____ ten _____ ones

5.

11
eleven

_____ ten _____ one

PROBLEM SOLVING REAL WORLD

Solve.

6. Tina thinks of a number that has 3 ones and 1 ten.
What is the number?

_____

Name _____

Lesson 56
COMMON CORE STANDARD CC.1.NBT.2c
Lesson Objective: Use objects, pictures, and numbers to represent tens.

Tens

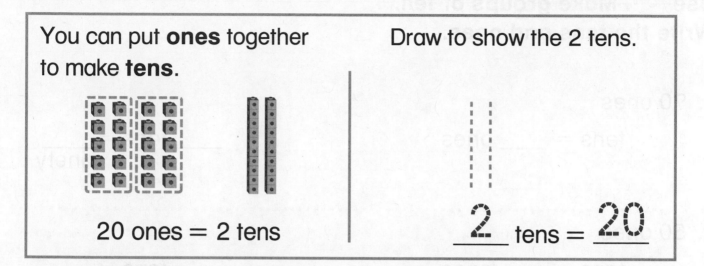

You can put **ones** together to make **tens**.

20 ones = 2 tens

Draw to show the 2 tens.

__2__ tens = __20__

Use 🔳. Make groups of ten. Draw the tens.
Write how many tens. Write the number.

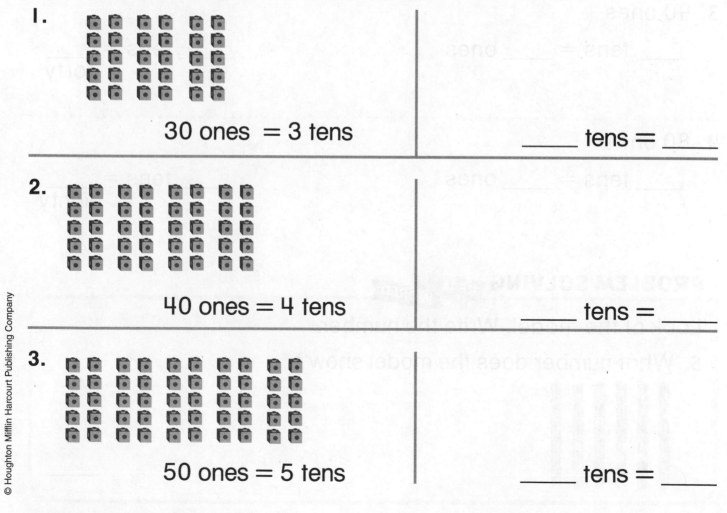

1. 30 ones = 3 tens

____ tens = ____

2. 40 ones = 4 tens

____ tens = ____

3. 50 ones = 5 tens

____ tens = ____

Tens

Use 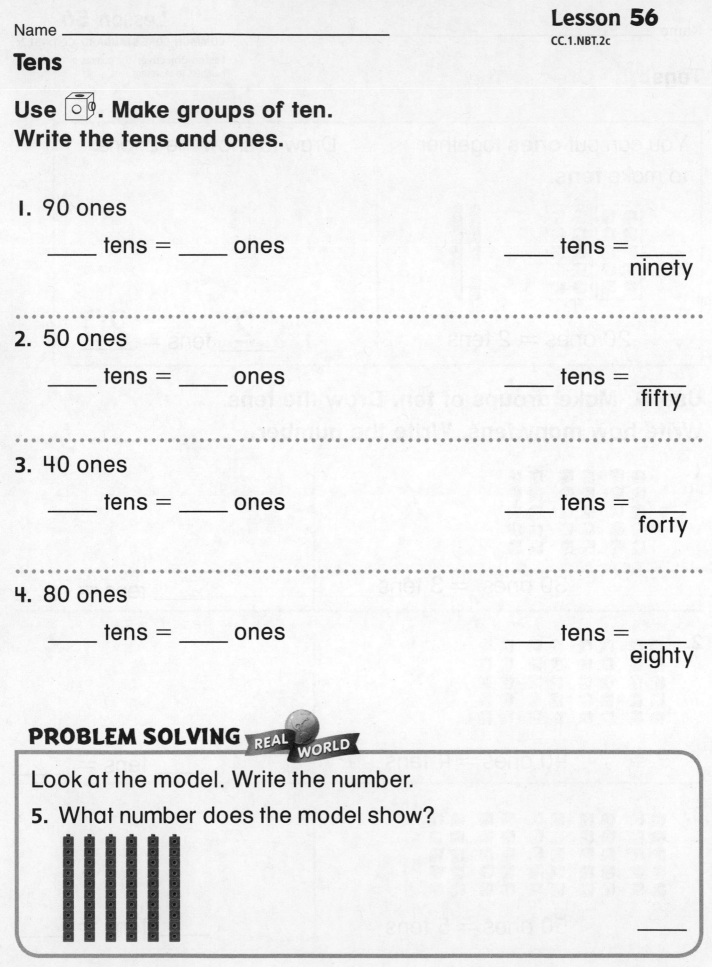. Make groups of ten.
Write the tens and ones.

1. 90 ones

____ tens = ____ ones

____ tens = ____
ninety

2. 50 ones

____ tens = ____ ones

____ tens = ____
fifty

3. 40 ones

____ tens = ____ ones

____ tens = ____
forty

4. 80 ones

____ tens = ____ ones

____ tens = ____
eighty

PROBLEM SOLVING REAL WORLD

Look at the model. Write the number.

5. What number does the model show?

____

Name _____

Lesson 57
COMMON CORE STANDARD CC.1.NBT.3
Lesson Objective: Model and compare two-digit numbers to determine which is greater.

Algebra • Greater Than

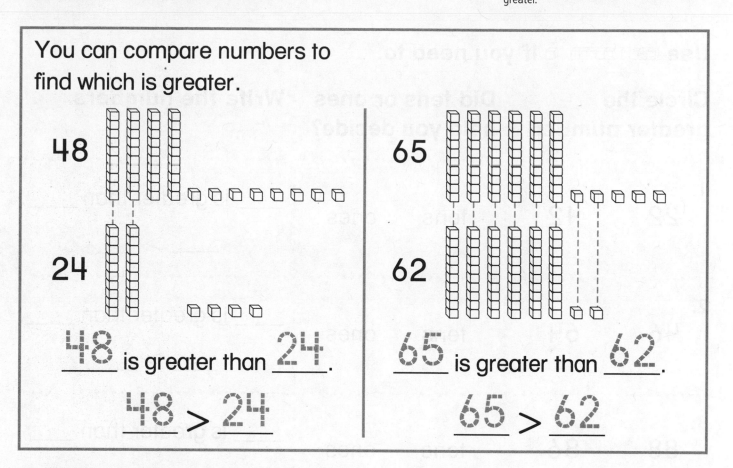

You can compare numbers to find which is greater.

48

24

__48__ is greater than __24__.

__48__ > __24__

65

62

__65__ is greater than __62__.

__65__ > __62__

Draw lines to match.
Write the numbers to compare.

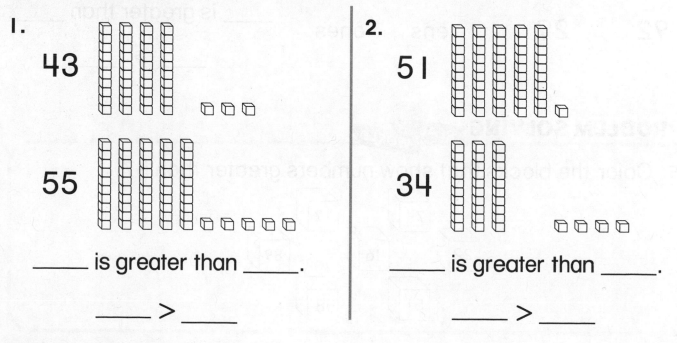

1.

43

55

_____ is greater than _____.

_____ > _____

2.

51

34

_____ is greater than _____.

_____ > _____

Number and Operations in Base Ten

Algebra • Greater Than

Use ▭▭▭ ▢ if you need to.

Circle the greater number.	Did tens or ones help you decide?	Write the numbers.
1. 22 42	tens ones	____ is greater than ____. ____ > ____
2. 46 64	tens ones	____ is greater than ____. ____ > ____
3. 88 86	tens ones	____ is greater than ____. ____ > ____
4. 92 29	tens ones	____ is greater than ____. ____ > ____

PROBLEM SOLVING REAL WORLD

5. Color the blocks that show numbers greater than 47.

74   17

22   46   89

51   48

Algebra • Less Than

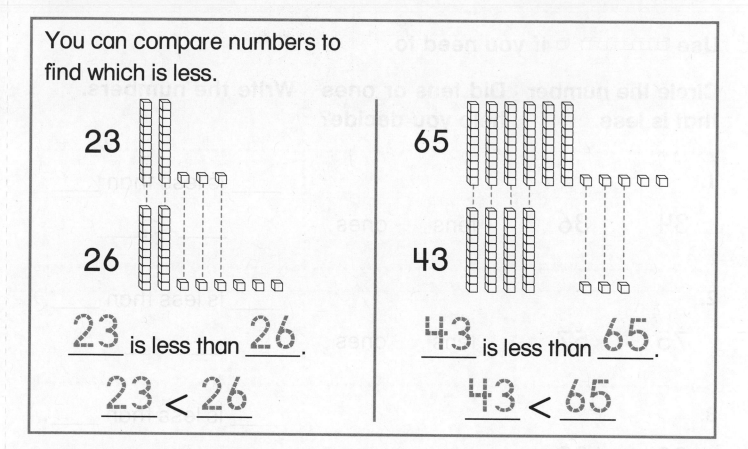

You can compare numbers to find which is less.

23

26

___23___ is less than ___26___ .

__23__ < __26__

65

43

___43___ is less than ___65___ .

__43__ < __65__

Draw lines to match.
Write the numbers to compare.

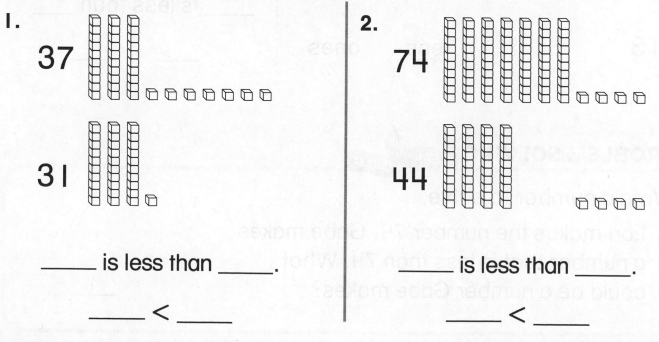

I.

37

31

_____ is less than _____ .

_____ < _____

2.

74

44

_____ is less than _____ .

_____ < _____

Number and Operations in Base Ten

Algebra • Less Than

Use ⬚⬚⬚⬚⬚ ⬚ if you need to.

Circle the number that is less.	Did tens or ones help you decide?	Write the numbers.
1. 34 36	tens ones	____ is less than ____. ____ < ____
2. 75 57	tens ones	____ is less than ____. ____ < ____
3. 80 89	tens ones	____ is less than ____. ____ < ____
4. 13 31	tens ones	____ is less than ____. ____ < ____

PROBLEM SOLVING REAL WORLD

Write a number to solve.

5. Lori makes the number 74. Gabe makes a number that is less than 74. What could be a number Gabe makes? ____

Algebra • Use Symbols to Compare

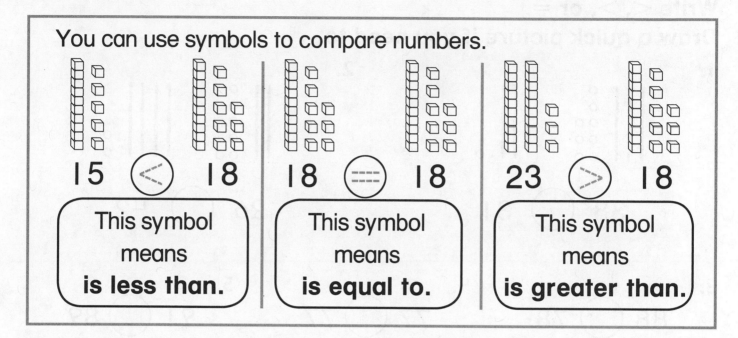

You can use symbols to compare numbers.

15 < 18   18 = 18   23 > 18

This symbol means **is less than.**

This symbol means **is equal to.**

This symbol means **is greater than.**

Write >, <, or =. Complete the sentence.

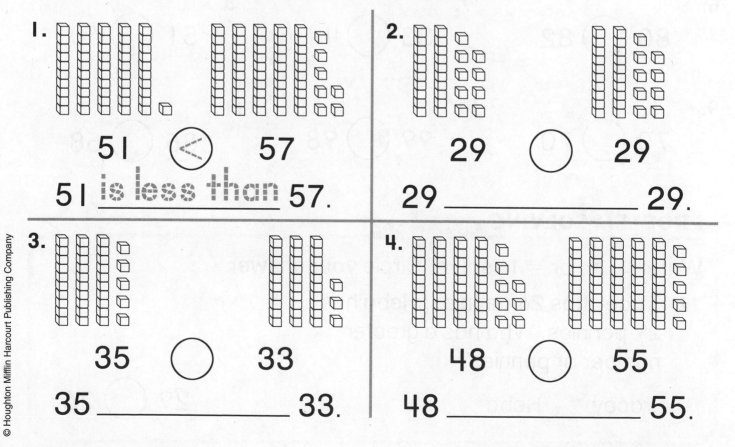

1. 51 < 57

   51 is less than 57.

2. 29 ◯ 29

   29 _____ 29.

3. 35 ◯ 33

   35 _____ 33.

4. 48 ◯ 55

   48 _____ 55.

Algebra • Use Symbols to Compare

Write <, >, or =.
Draw a quick picture if you need to.

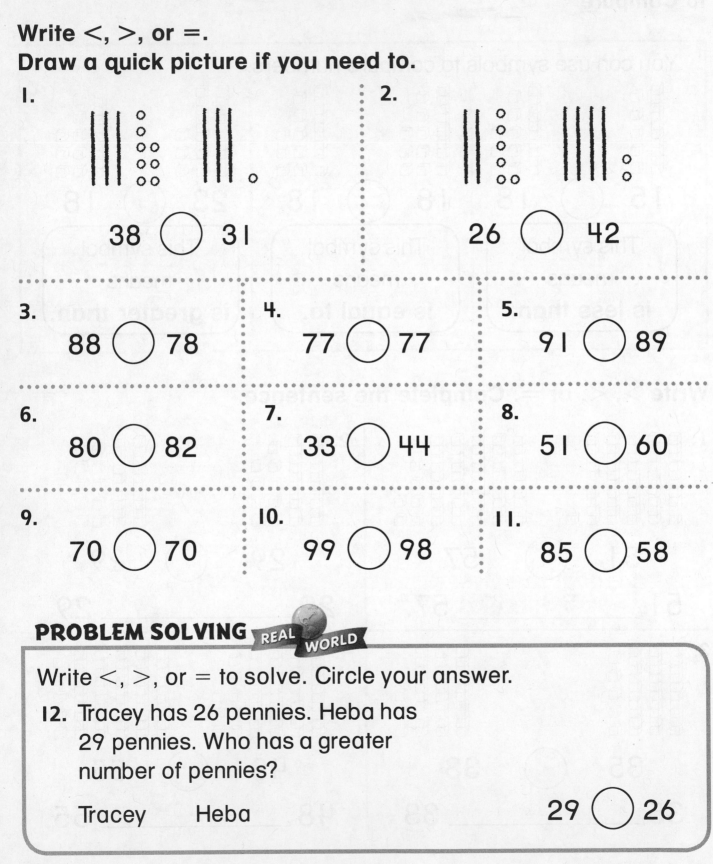

1.

38 ◯ 31

2.

26 ◯ 42

3. 88 ◯ 78

4. 77 ◯ 77

5. 91 ◯ 89

6. 80 ◯ 82

7. 33 ◯ 44

8. 51 ◯ 60

9. 70 ◯ 70

10. 99 ◯ 98

11. 85 ◯ 58

PROBLEM SOLVING REAL WORLD

Write <, >, or = to solve. Circle your answer.

12. Tracey has 26 pennies. Heba has 29 pennies. Who has a greater number of pennies?

Tracey   Heba

29 ◯ 26

Name _____

Lesson 60
COMMON CORE STANDARD CC.1.NBT.3
Lesson Objective: Solve problems using the strategy *make a model*.

Problem Solving • Compare Numbers

Anthony has the number cards shown. He gives away the cards with numbers less than 6 and greater than 9. Which cards does Anthony have now?

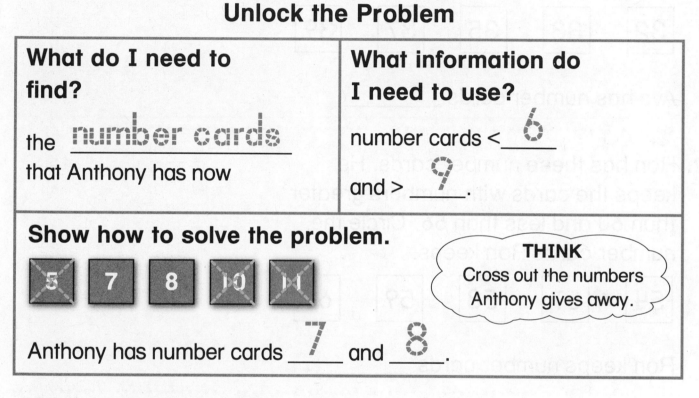

Unlock the Problem

What do I need to find?	**What information do I need to use?**
the <u>number cards</u> that Anthony has now	number cards < _6_ and > _9_.

Show how to solve the problem.

Anthony has number cards _7_ and _8_.

THINK
Cross out the numbers Anthony gives away.

Make a model to solve.

1. Emily has the number cards shown. She gives away the cards less than 19 and greater than 22. Which cards does she have now?

Emily has _____ and _____.

Problem Solving •
Compare Numbers

Make a model to solve.

1. Ava has these number cards. She gives away cards with numbers less than 34 and greater than 38. Which number cards does Ava have now?

| 32 | 33 | 35 | 37 | 39 |

Ava has number cards _____.

2. Ron has these number cards. He keeps the cards with numbers greater than 60 and less than 56. Circle the number cards Ron keeps.

| 54 | 57 | 58 | 59 | 61 |

Ron keeps number cards _____.

3. Mia has these number cards. She keeps the cards with numbers less than 85 and greater than 88. Circle the cards Mia keeps.

| 84 | 86 | 87 | 89 | 90 |

Mia keeps number cards _____.

Name _____

Lesson 61

COMMON CORE STANDARD CC.1.NBT.4
Lesson Objective: Draw a model to add tens.

Add Tens

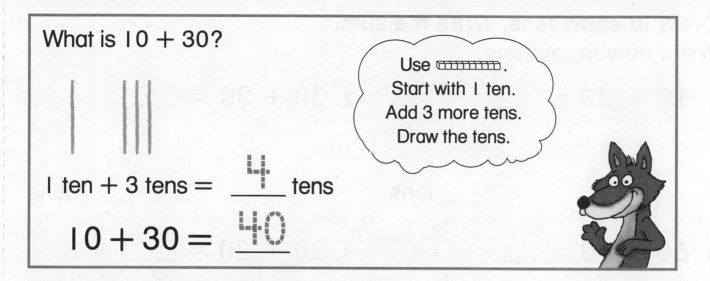

What is $10 + 30$?

1 ten + 3 tens = ____ **4** tens

$10 + 30 =$ **40**

Use ▭. Start with 1 ten. Add 3 more tens. Draw the tens.

Use ▭. Draw to show tens.
Write how many tens. Write the sum.

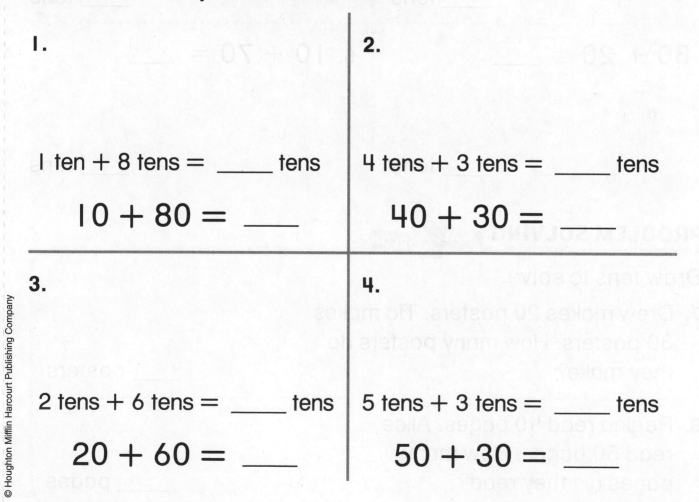

1.

1 ten + 8 tens = _____ tens

$10 + 80 =$ ___

2.

4 tens + 3 tens = _____ tens

$40 + 30 =$ ___

3.

2 tens + 6 tens = _____ tens

$20 + 60 =$ ___

4.

5 tens + 3 tens = _____ tens

$50 + 30 =$ ___

Add Tens

Draw to show tens. Write the sum.
Write how many tens.

1. $10 + 30 =$ ___

___ tens

2. $30 + 30 =$ ___

___ tens

3. $60 + 10 =$ ___

___ tens

4. $20 + 20 =$ ___

___ tens

5. $30 + 20 =$ ___

___ tens

6. $10 + 70 =$ ___

___ tens

PROBLEM SOLVING REAL WORLD

Draw tens to solve.

7. Drew makes 20 posters. Tia makes 30 posters. How many posters do they make?

___ posters

8. Regina read 40 pages. Alice read 50 pages. How many pages did they read?

___ pages

Name _____

Lesson 62
COMMON CORE STANDARD CC.1.NBT.4
Lesson Objective: Use a hundred chart to find sums.

Use a Hundred Chart to Add

You can count on to add on a hundred chart.

1	2	3	4	5	6	7	8	9	10
11	12	13	14	15	16	17	18	19	20
21	22	23	24	25	26	27	28	29	30
31	32	33	34	35	36	37	38	39	40
41	42	43	44	45	46	47	48	49	50
51	52	53	54	55	56	57	58	59	60
61	62	63	64	65	66	67	68	69	70
71	72	73	74	75	76	77	78	79	80
81	82	83	84	85	86	87	88	89	90
91	92	93	94	95	96	97	98	99	100

Start at 21. Move right to count on 3 ones. Count

22, 23, 24

$21 + 3 = 24$

Start at 68. Move down to count on 3 tens. Count

78, 88, 98

$68 + 30 = 98$

Use the hundred chart to add.
Count on by ones.

1. $46 + 2 = $ _____

2. $63 + 3 = $ _____

Count on by tens.

3. $52 + 30 = $ _____

4. $23 + 40 = $ _____

Use a Hundred Chart to Add

**Use the hundred chart to add.
Count on by ones or tens.**

1. $47 + 2 =$ ____

2. $26 + 50 =$ ____

3. $22 + 5 =$ ____

4. $40 + 41 =$ ____

5. $4 + 85 =$ ____

1	2	3	4	5	6	7	8	9	10
11	12	13	14	15	16	17	18	19	20
21	22	23	24	25	26	27	28	29	30
31	32	33	34	35	36	37	38	39	40
41	42	43	44	45	46	47	48	49	50
51	52	53	54	55	56	57	58	59	60
61	62	63	64	65	66	67	68	69	70
71	72	73	74	75	76	77	78	79	80
81	82	83	84	85	86	87	88	89	90
91	92	93	94	95	96	97	98	99	100

PROBLEM SOLVING REAL WORLD

Choose a way to solve. Draw or write to show your work.

6. 17 children are on the bus. Then 20 more children get on the bus. How many children are on the bus now?

____ children

Name _____

Lesson 63

COMMON CORE STANDARD CC.1.NBT.4
Lesson Objective: Use concrete models to add ones or tens to a two-digit number.

Use Models to Add

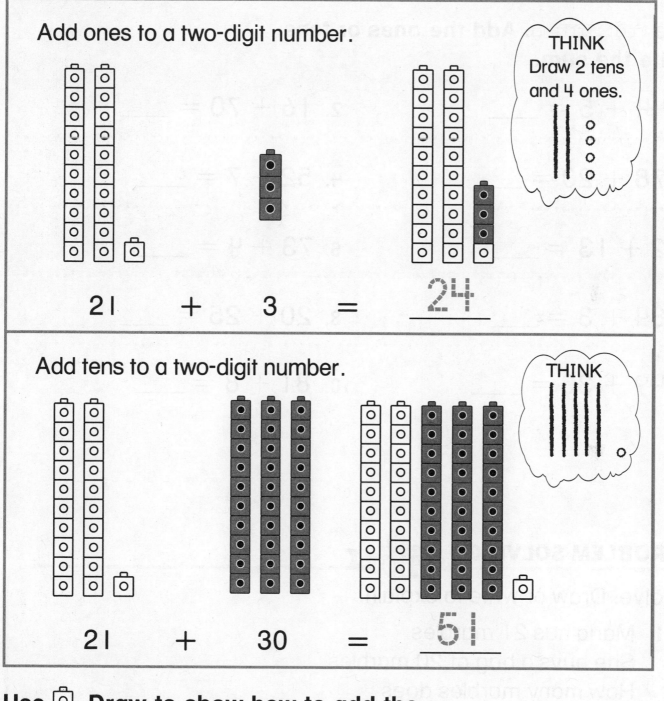

Add ones to a two-digit number.

THINK
Draw 2 tens and 4 ones.

21   +   3   =   24

Add tens to a two-digit number.

THINK

21   +   30   =   51

Use ▢. Draw to show how to add the ones or tens. Write the sum.

1. 15 + 2 = _____

2. 15 + 20 = _____

Use Models to Add

Use ⬚⬚⬚⬚⬚⬚ ▢. Add the ones or tens.
Write the sum.

1. $44 + 5 =$ ___

2. $16 + 70 =$ ___

3. $78 + 20 =$ ___

4. $52 + 7 =$ ___

5. $2 + 13 =$ ___

6. $73 + 4 =$ ___

7. $84 + 3 =$ ___

8. $20 + 25 =$ ___

9. $49 + 30 =$ ___

10. $81 + 8 =$ ___

PROBLEM SOLVING REAL WORLD

Solve. Draw or write to explain.

11. Maria has 21 marbles.
    She buys a bag of 20 marbles.
    How many marbles does
    Maria have now?

____ marbles

Lesson 64

COMMON CORE STANDARD CC.1.NBT.4

Lesson Objective: Make a ten to add a two-digit number and a one-digit number.

Make Ten to Add

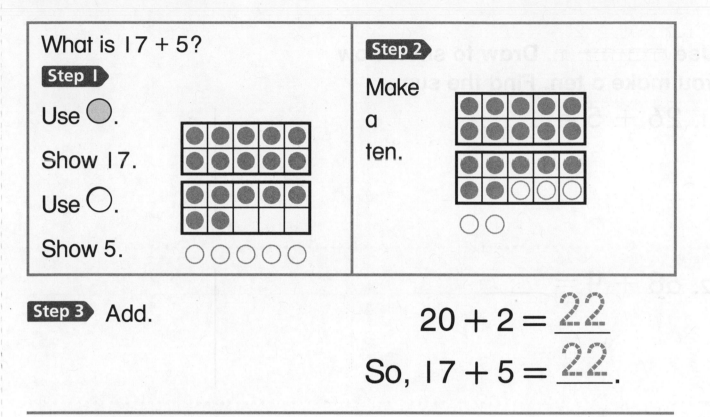

What is 17 + 5?

Step 1

Use ⬤.

Show 17.

Use ◯.

Show 5.

Step 2

Make a ten.

Step 3 Add.

$$20 + 2 = \underline{22}$$

So, $17 + 5 = \underline{22}$.

Draw to show how you make a ten. Find the sum.

1. What is 16 + 8?

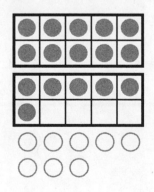

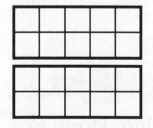

$$\underline{20} + \underline{4} = \underline{24}$$

So, $16 + 8 = \underline{}$.

Make Ten to Add

Use ▭▭▭▭ ▭. **Draw to show how you make a ten. Find the sum.**

1. 26 + 5 = ____

2. 68 + 4 = ____

3. 35 + 8 = ____

PROBLEM SOLVING

Choose a way to solve. Draw or write to show your work.

4. Debbie has 27 markers. Sal has 9 markers. How many markers do they have?

____ markers

Name _____

Lesson 65
COMMON CORE STANDARD CC.1.NBT.4
Lesson Objective: Use tens and ones to add two-digit numbers.

Use Place Value to Add

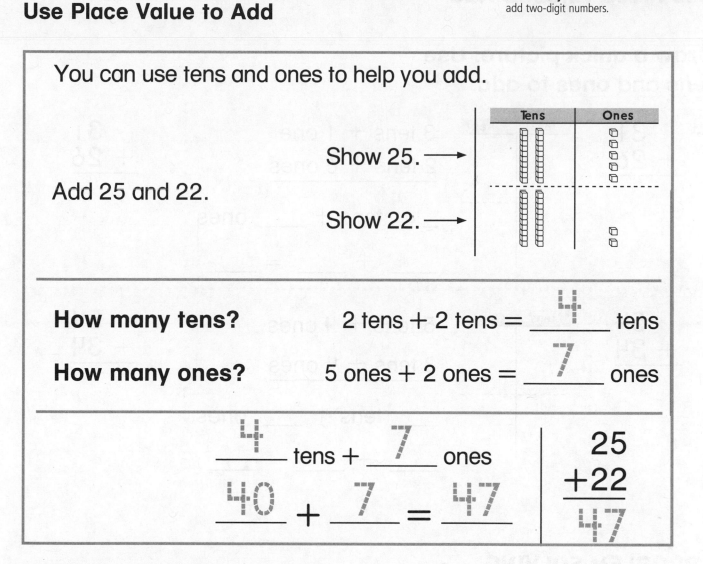

You can use tens and ones to help you add.

Add 25 and 22.

Show 25. ⟶

Show 22. ⟶

Tens	Ones

How many tens?   2 tens + 2 tens = ___4___ tens

How many ones?   5 ones + 2 ones = ___7___ ones

___4___ tens + ___7___ ones

___40___ + ___7___ = ___47___

$\begin{array}{r} 25 \\ +22 \\ \hline 47 \end{array}$

Use tens and ones to add.

I. Add 34 and 42.

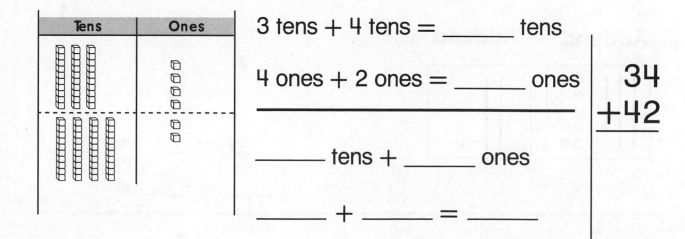

Tens	Ones

3 tens + 4 tens = _____ tens

4 ones + 2 ones = _____ ones

_____ tens + _____ ones

_____ + _____ = _____

$\begin{array}{r} 34 \\ +42 \\ \hline \end{array}$

Use Place Value to Add

Draw a quick picture. Use tens and ones to add.

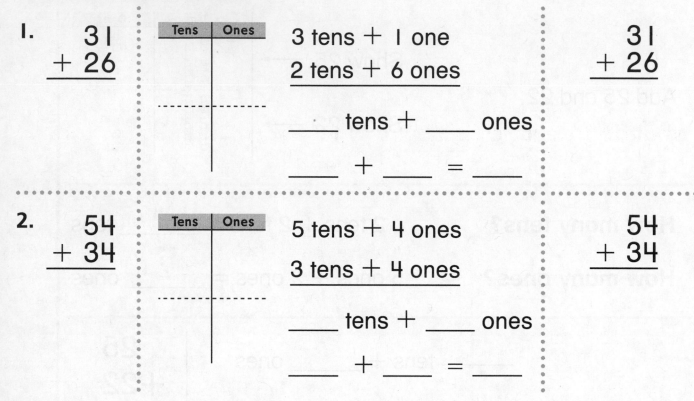

1. $\begin{array}{r} 31 \\ + 26 \\ \hline \end{array}$

Tens	Ones

3 tens + 1 one
2 tens + 6 ones

___ tens + ___ ones

___ + ___ = ___

$\begin{array}{r} 31 \\ + 26 \\ \hline \end{array}$

2. $\begin{array}{r} 54 \\ + 34 \\ \hline \end{array}$

Tens	Ones

5 tens + 4 ones
3 tens + 4 ones

___ tens + ___ ones

___ + ___ = ___

$\begin{array}{r} 54 \\ + 34 \\ \hline \end{array}$

PROBLEM SOLVING

3. Write two addition sentences you can use to find the sum. Then solve.

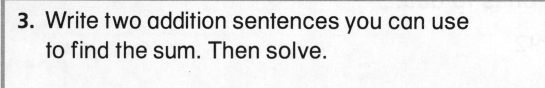

Addend   **Addend**

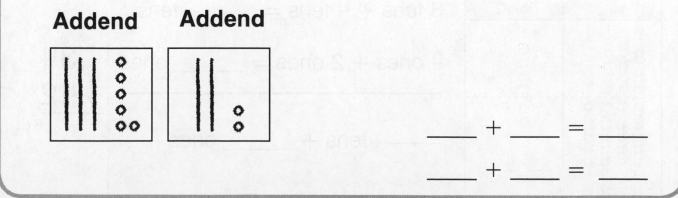

___ + ___ = ___

___ + ___ = ___

Lesson 66

COMMON CORE STANDARD CC.1.NBT.4
Lesson Objective: Solve and explain
two-digit addition word problems using the
strategy *draw a picture.*

Problem Solving • Addition
Word Problems

Morgan plants 17 seeds.

Amy plants 8 seeds.

How many seeds do they plant?

Unlock the Problem

What do I need to find?	What information do I need to use?
how many ~~seeds~~ they plant	Morgan plants __17__ seeds. Amy plants __8__ seeds.

Show how to solve the problem.

count on ones

(make a ten)

add tens and ones

____ seeds.

Draw to solve. Circle your reasoning.

1. Edward buys 24 tomato plants.
   He buys 15 pepper plants.
   How many plants does he buy?

   count on tens
   make a ten
   add tens and ones

   ____ plants

Problem Solving • Addition Word Problems

Draw and write to solve. Explain your reasoning.

1. Dale saved 19 pennies. Then he found 5 more pennies. How many pennies does Dale have now?

_____

_____

_____

_____ pennies

2. Jean has 10 fish. She gets 4 more fish. How many fish does she have now?

_____

_____

_____

_____ fish

3. Courtney buys 2 bags of apples. Each bag has 20 apples. How many apples does she buy?

_____

_____

_____

_____ apples

4. John bakes 18 blueberry muffins and 12 banana muffins for the bake sale. How many muffins does he bake?

_____

_____

_____

_____ muffins

Name _____

Lesson 67

COMMON CORE STANDARD CC.1.NBT.5

Lesson Objective: Identify numbers that are
10 less or 10 more than a given number.

10 Less, 10 More

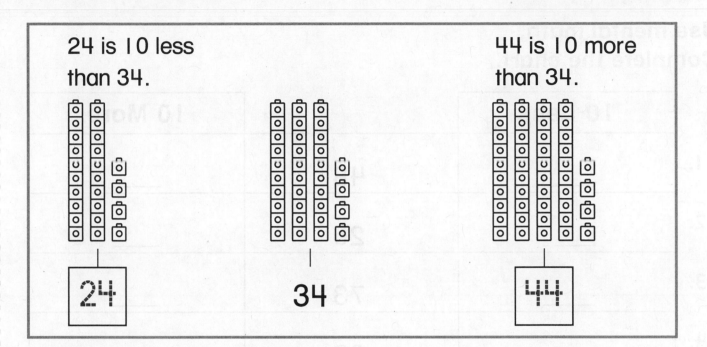

24 is 10 less
than 34.

44 is 10 more
than 34.

24   34   44

Write the numbers that are
10 less and 10 more.

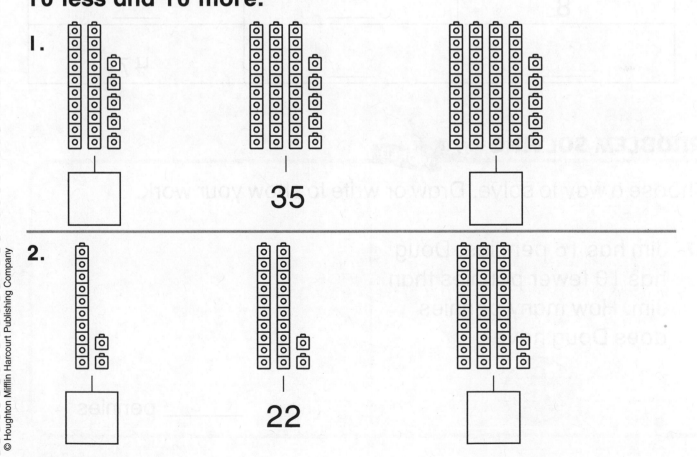

1.

35

2.

22

10 Less, 10 More

Use mental math.
Complete the chart.

	10 Less		10 More
1.	___	48	___
2.	___	25	___
3.	___	73	___
4.	___	89	___
5.	8	___	___
6.	___	___	47

PROBLEM SOLVING REAL WORLD

Choose a way to solve. Draw or write to show your work.

7. Jim has 16 pennies. Doug
   has 10 fewer pennies than
   Jim. How many pennies
   does Doug have?

_____ pennies

134

Subtract Tens

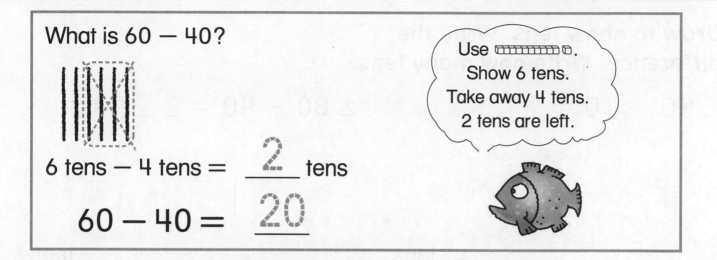

What is 60 − 40?

6 tens − 4 tens = __2__ tens

60 − 40 = __20__

Use ▭. Show 6 tens. Take away 4 tens. 2 tens are left.

Use ▭. Draw to show tens.
Write how many tens. Write the difference.

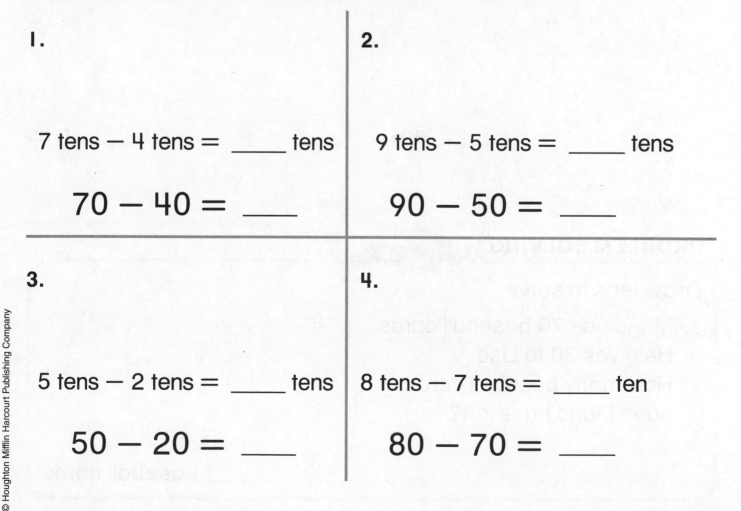

1.

7 tens − 4 tens = ____ tens

70 − 40 = ___

2.

9 tens − 5 tens = ____ tens

90 − 50 = ___

3.

5 tens − 2 tens = ____ tens

50 − 20 = ___

4.

8 tens − 7 tens = ____ ten

80 − 70 = ___

Subtract Tens

Draw to show tens. Write the difference. Write how many tens.

1. $40 - 10 = $ ___

_____ tens

2. $80 - 40 = $ ___

_____ tens

3. $50 - 30 = $ ___

_____ tens

4. $60 - 30 = $ ___

_____ tens

PROBLEM SOLVING REAL WORLD

Draw tens to solve.

5. Mario has 70 baseball cards.
He gives 30 to Lisa.
How many baseball cards
does Mario have left?

_____ baseball cards

Name _____

Lesson 69

COMMON CORE STANDARD CC.1.NBT.6
Lesson Objective: Add and subtract within
100, including continued practice with facts
within 20.

Practice Addition and Subtraction

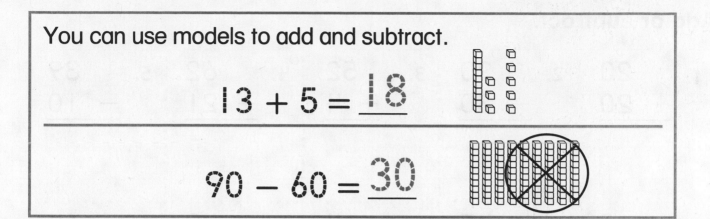

You can use models to add and subtract.

$13 + 5 = \underline{18}$

$90 - 60 = \underline{30}$

Add or subtract.

1. $33 + 6 =$ ___	2. $10 + 10 =$ ___	3. $15 - 8 =$ ___
4. $6 + 7 =$ ___	5. $54 + 23 =$ ___	6. $71 + 8 =$ ___
7. $5 + 5 =$ ___	8. $8 - 8 =$ ___	9. $16 + 3 =$ ___
10. $55 + 12 =$ ___	11. $9 - 7 =$ ___	12. $30 - 10 =$ ___

Practice Addition and Subtraction

Add or subtract.

1. $\begin{array}{r} 20 \\ + 20 \\ \hline \end{array}$ 2. $\begin{array}{r} 90 \\ - 30 \\ \hline \end{array}$ 3. $\begin{array}{r} 52 \\ + 4 \\ \hline \end{array}$ 4. $\begin{array}{r} 62 \\ + 21 \\ \hline \end{array}$ 5. $\begin{array}{r} 39 \\ - 10 \\ \hline \end{array}$

6. $\begin{array}{r} 8 \\ + 2 \\ \hline \end{array}$ 7. $\begin{array}{r} 47 \\ + 34 \\ \hline \end{array}$ 8. $\begin{array}{r} 4 \\ - 0 \\ \hline \end{array}$ 9. $\begin{array}{r} 49 \\ - 6 \\ \hline \end{array}$ 10. $\begin{array}{r} 64 \\ + 30 \\ \hline \end{array}$

11. $\begin{array}{r} 63 \\ + 11 \\ \hline \end{array}$ 12. $\begin{array}{r} 37 \\ - 6 \\ \hline \end{array}$ 13. $\begin{array}{r} 85 \\ + 13 \\ \hline \end{array}$ 14. $\begin{array}{r} 48 \\ + 11 \\ \hline \end{array}$ 15. $\begin{array}{r} 76 \\ - 15 \\ \hline \end{array}$

PROBLEM SOLVING REAL WORLD

Solve. Write or draw to explain.

16. Andrew read 17 pages of his book before dinner. He read 9 more pages after dinner. How many pages did he read?

_____ pages

Order Length

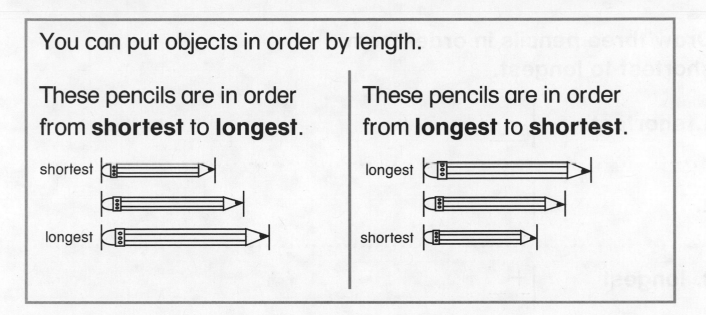

You can put objects in order by length.

These pencils are in order from **shortest** to **longest**.

shortest

longest

These pencils are in order from **longest** to **shortest**.

longest

shortest

Draw three lines in order from **shortest** to **longest**.

I. shortest |

2. |

3. longest |

Draw three lines in order from **longest** to **shortest**.

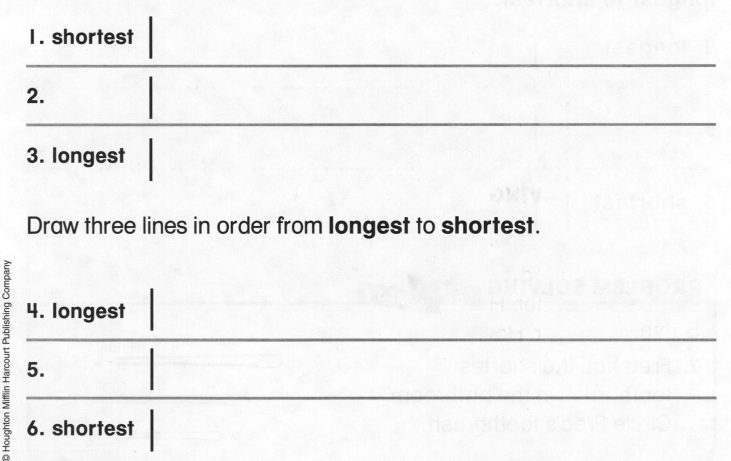

4. longest |

5. |

6. shortest |

Order Length

Draw three pencils in order from shortest to longest.

1. shortest |

2. |

3. longest |

Draw three markers in order from longest to shortest.

4. longest |

5. |

6. shortest |

PROBLEM SOLVING REAL WORLD

Solve.

7. Fred has the shortest toothbrush in the bathroom. Circle Fred's toothbrush.

Name _____

Lesson 71
COMMON CORE STANDARD CC.1.MD.1
Lesson Objective: Use the transitivity principle to measure indirectly.

Indirect Measurement

Clue 1: A marker is shorter than a pencil.
Clue 2: The pencil is shorter than a ribbon.

Is the marker shorter or longer than the ribbon?

marker

pencil

ribbon

So, the marker is __shorter__ than the ribbon.

> Draw Clue 1.
> Draw Clue 2.
> Then compare the marker and the ribbon.

Use the clues. Write **shorter** or **longer** to complete the sentence. Then draw to prove your answer.

> Draw Clue 1.
> Draw Clue 2.
> Then compare the string and the pencil.

1. Clue 1: A string is longer than a straw.
   Clue 2: The straw is longer than a pencil.
   Is the string shorter or longer than the pencil?

string

straw

pencil

The string is _____ than the pencil.

Measurement and Data

Name _____

Indirect Measurement

Read the clues. Write shorter or longer to complete the sentence. Then draw to prove your answer.

1. Clue 1: A yarn is longer than a ribbon.

   Clue 2: The ribbon is longer than a crayon.

   So, the yarn is _____ than the crayon.

yarn

_____

ribbon

_____

crayon

PROBLEM SOLVING REAL WORLD

Solve. Draw or write to explain.

2. Megan's pencil is shorter than Tasha's pencil.

   Tasha's pencil is shorter than Kim's pencil.

   Is Megan's pencil shorter or longer than Kim's pencil?

   _____

Use Nonstandard Units to Measure Length

You can use ■ to measure length.

Line up the ■.

Count how many.

about __5__ ■

Use real objects. Use ■ to measure.

Count how many.

1. Crayons NON-TOXIC

about _____ ■

2. Glue

about _____ ■

3.

about _____ ■

4.

about _____ ■

Measurement and Data

Name _____

Use Nonstandard Units to Measure Length

Use real objects. Use to measure.

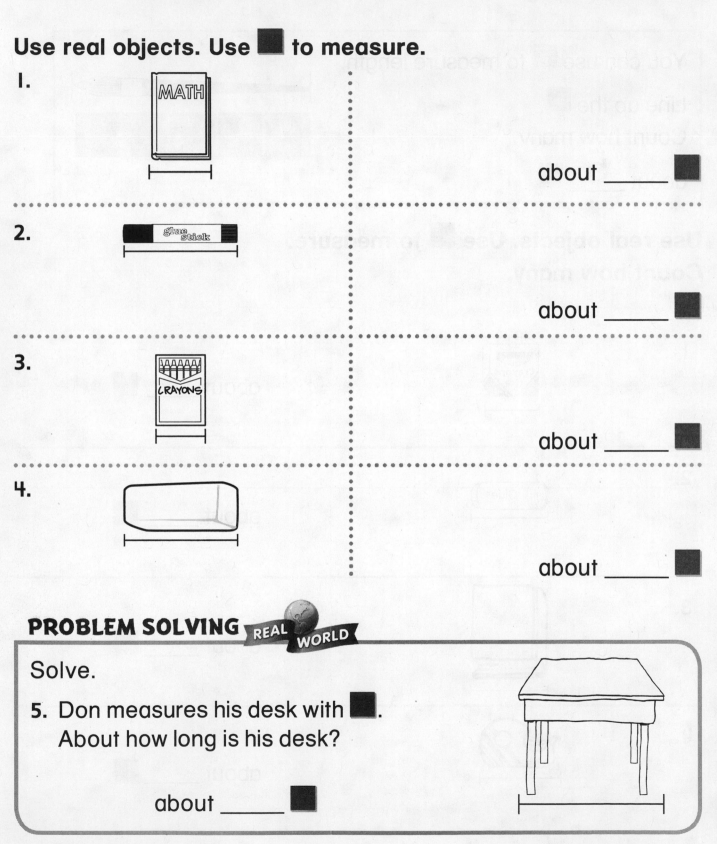

1. MATH

   about _____ ▪

2. glue stick

   about _____ ▪

3. CRAYONS

   about _____ ▪

4.

   about _____ ▪

PROBLEM SOLVING REAL WORLD

Solve.

5. Don measures his desk with ▪.
   About how long is his desk?

   about _____ ▪

Make a Nonstandard Measuring Tool

About how long is the ribbon?
Count to measure.

10
_____

Count on by ones.

about _____ ⌐◯

**Use real objects and the measuring tool you made.
Measure.**

1. MATH

about _____ ⌐◯

2.

about _____ ⌐◯

3.

about _____ ⌐◯

Make a Nonstandard Measuring Tool

Use the measuring tool you made.
Measure real objects.

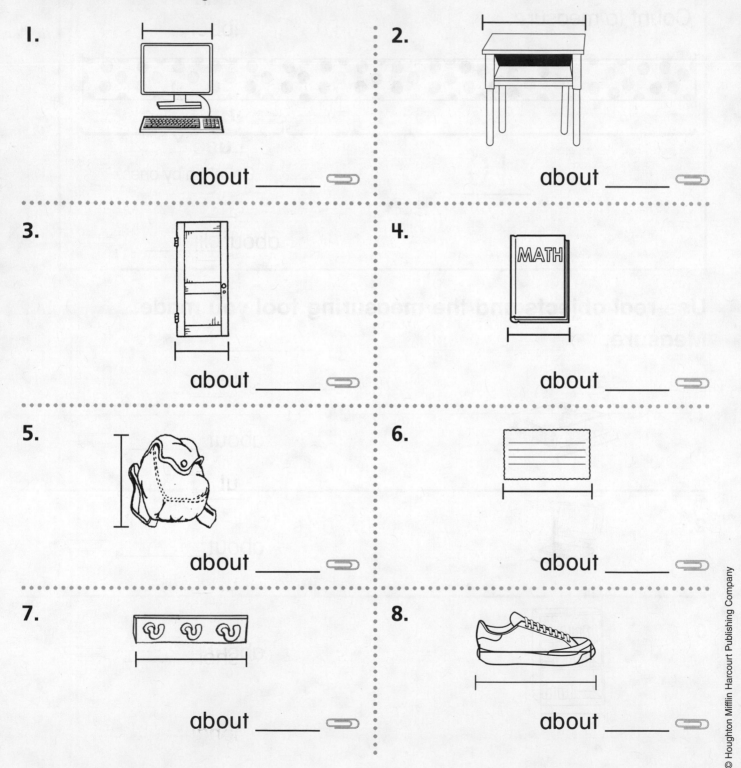

1.

about _____ ⌒

2.

about _____ ⌒

3.

about _____ ⌒

4.

about _____ ⌒

5.

about _____ ⌒

6.

about _____ ⌒

7.

about _____ ⌒

8.

about _____ ⌒

Lesson 74

COMMON CORE STANDARD CC.1.MD.2

Lesson Objective: Solve measurement problems using the strategy *act it out*.

Name _____

Problem Solving •
Measure and Compare

The gray ribbon is 3 ⬭ long. The white ribbon is
4 ⬭ long. The black ribbon is 1 ⬭ longer than the
white ribbon. Draw and color the length of the ribbons in
order from **shortest** to **longest**.

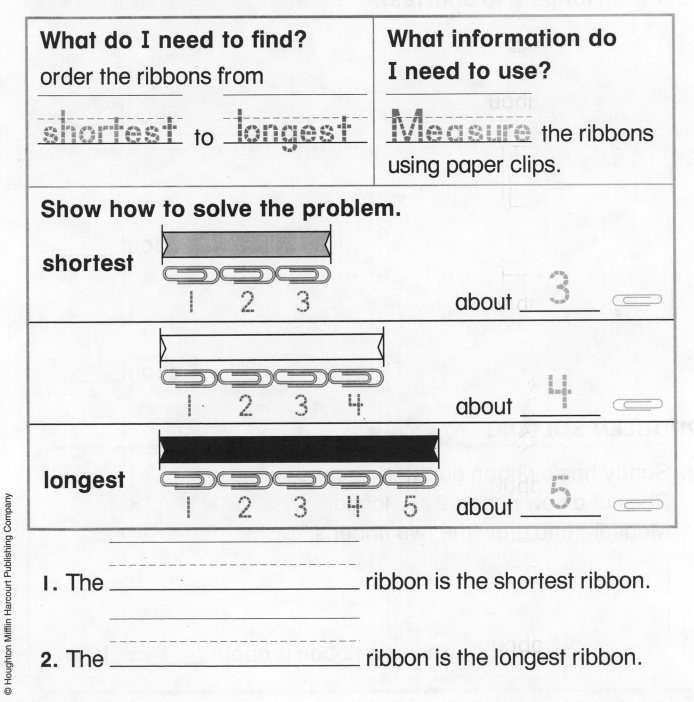

What do I need to find?	**What information do I need to use?**
order the ribbons from shortest to longest	Measure the ribbons using paper clips.

Show how to solve the problem.

shortest   1 2 3   about ___3___ ⬭

1 2 3 4   about ___4___ ⬭

longest   1 2 3 4 5   about ___5___ ⬭

1. The _____ ribbon is the shortest ribbon.

2. The _____ ribbon is the longest ribbon.

Problem Solving • Measure and Compare

The blue string is about 3 ⌕ long.
The green string is 2 ⌕ longer than the blue
string. The red string is 1 ⌕ shorter than the
blue string. Measure and draw the strings in
order from **longest** to **shortest**.

1. |

about _____ ⌕

2. |

about _____ ⌕

3. |

about _____ ⌕

PROBLEM SOLVING REAL WORLD

4. Sandy has a ribbon about 4 ⌕ long.
   She cut a new ribbon 2 ⌕ longer.
   Measure and draw the two ribbons.

   |
   |

   The new ribbon is about _____ ⌕ long.

Lesson 75

COMMON CORE STANDARD CC.1.MD.3

Lesson Objective: Write times to the hour shown on analog clocks.

Time to the Hour

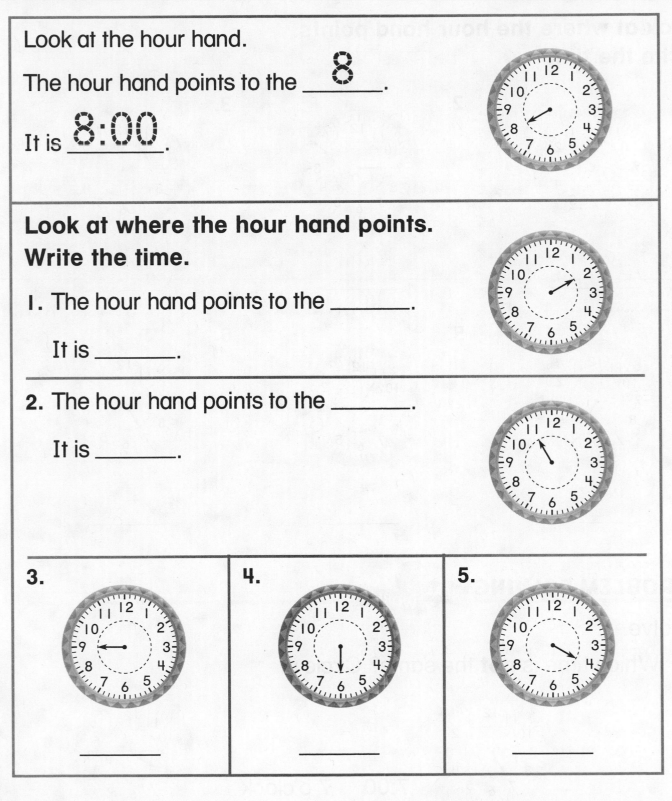

Look at the hour hand.

The hour hand points to the __**8**__.

It is __**8:00**__.

**Look at where the hour hand points.
Write the time.**

I. The hour hand points to the _____.

It is _____.

2. The hour hand points to the _____.

It is _____.

3.

_____

4.

_____

5.

_____

Measurement and Data

Time to the Hour

**Look at where the hour hand points.
Write the time.**

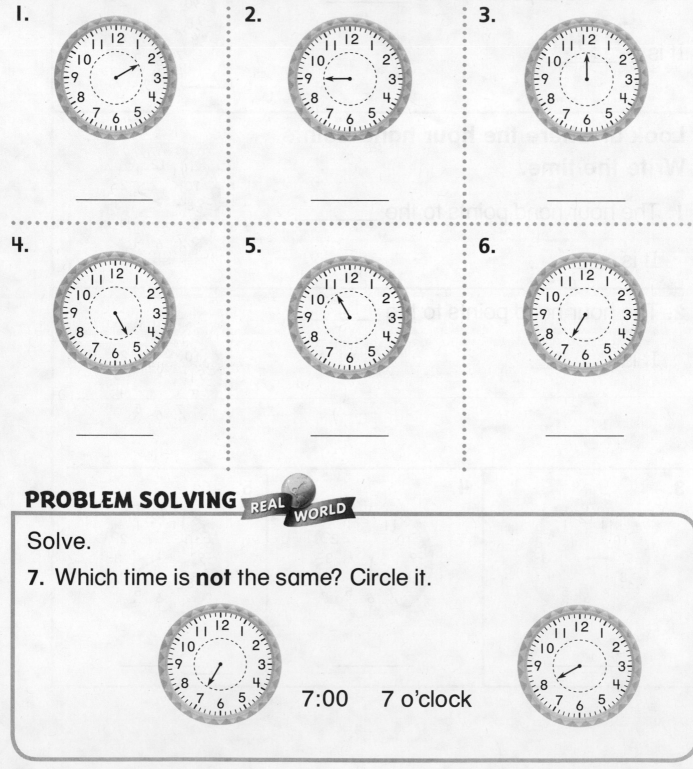

1.

_____

2.

_____

3.

_____

4.

_____

5.

_____

6.

_____

PROBLEM SOLVING REAL WORLD

Solve.

7. Which time is **not** the same? Circle it.

7:00   7 o'clock

Lesson 76

COMMON CORE STANDARD CC.1.MD.3
Lesson Objective: Write times to the half hour shown on analog clocks.

Time to the Half Hour

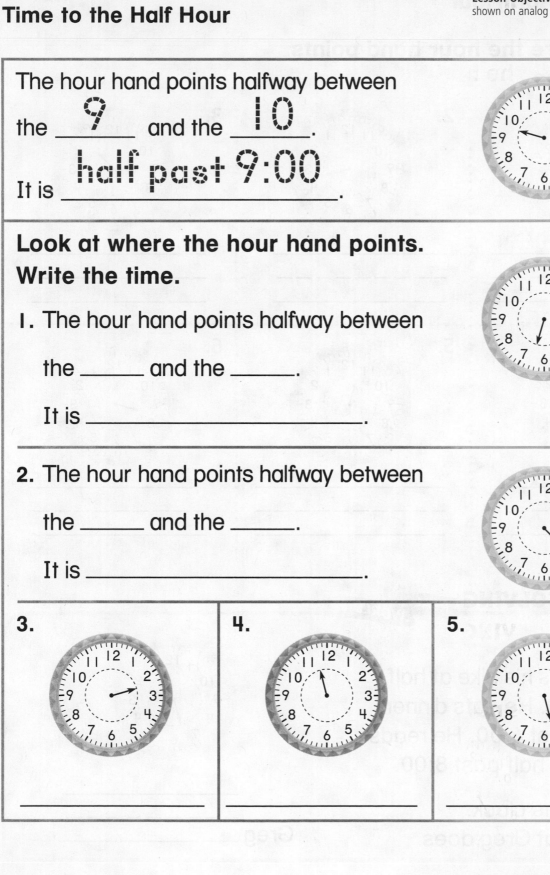

The hour hand points halfway between

the ___**9**___ and the ___**10**___.

It is ___half past 9:00___.

Look at where the hour hand points.
Write the time.

1. The hour hand points halfway between

   the _____ and the _____.

   It is _____.

2. The hour hand points halfway between

   the _____ and the _____.

   It is _____.

3.

_____

4.

_____

5.

_____

Measurement and Data

Time to the Half Hour

**Look at where the hour hand points.
Write the time.**

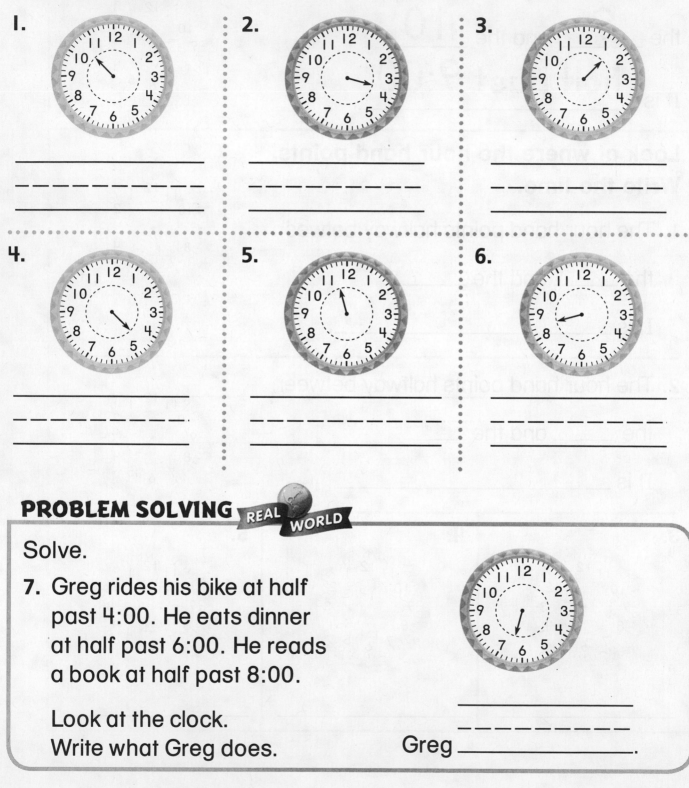

1.

_____

- - - - - - - - - -

_____

2.

_____

- - - - - - - - - -

_____

3.

_____

- - - - - - - - - -

_____

4.

_____

- - - - - - - - - -

_____

5.

_____

- - - - - - - - - -

_____

6.

_____

- - - - - - - - - -

_____

PROBLEM SOLVING REAL WORLD

Solve.

7. Greg rides his bike at half past 4:00. He eats dinner at half past 6:00. He reads a book at half past 8:00.

Look at the clock.
Write what Greg does.

_____

- - - - - - - - - -

Greg _____ .

Tell Time to the Hour and Half Hour

The short hand is the **hour hand**.
It shows the hour.

The long hand is the **minute hand**.
It shows the minutes after the hour.

There are 60 minutes in one hour.

8:00

There are 30 minutes in a half hour.

8:30

Write the time.

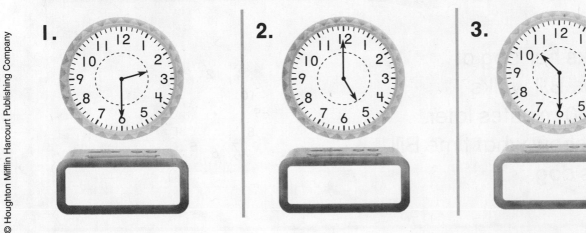

1.

2.

3.

Tell Time to the Hour and Half Hour

Write the time.

1.

2.

3.

4.

5.

6.

PROBLEM SOLVING **REAL WORLD**

Solve.

7. Lulu walks her dog at 7 o'clock. Bill walks his dog 30 minutes later. Draw to show what time Bill walks his dog.

Name _____

Lesson 78

COMMON CORE STANDARD CC.1.MD.3
Lesson Objective: Use the hour hand to draw
and write times on analog and digital clocks.

Practice Time to the Hour and Half Hour

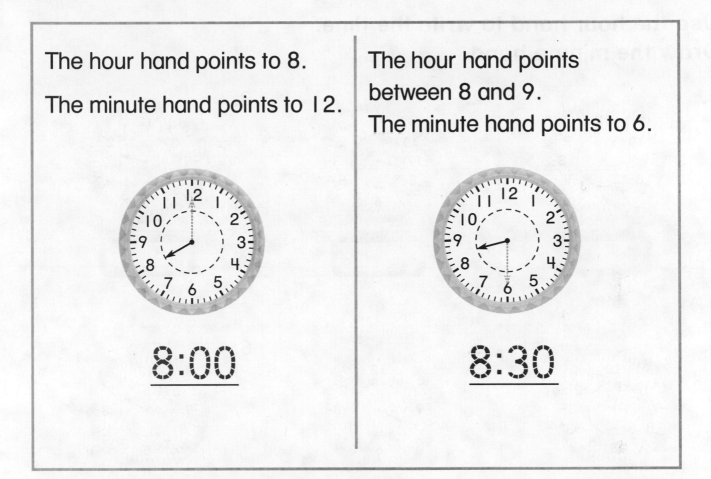

The hour hand points to 8.

The minute hand points to 12.

8:00

The hour hand points between 8 and 9.

The minute hand points to 6.

8:30

Use the hour hand to write the time.
Draw the minute hand.

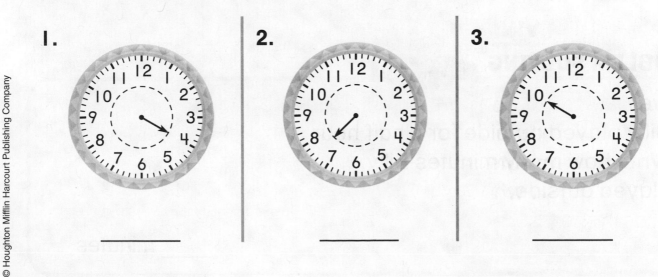

1.

_____

2.

_____

3.

_____

Practice Time to the Hour and Half Hour

**Use the hour hand to write the time.
Draw the minute hand.**

1.

2.

3.

4.

5.

6.

PROBLEM SOLVING REAL WORLD

Solve.

7. Billy played outside for a half hour.
   Write how many minutes Billy
   played outside.

_____ minutes

Name _____

Lesson 79

COMMON CORE STANDARD CC.1.MD.4

Lesson Objective: Analyze and compare data shown in a picture graph where each symbol represents one.

Read Picture Graphs

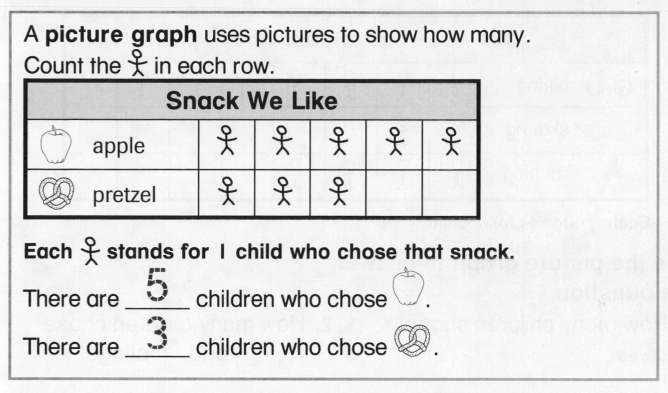

A **picture graph** uses pictures to show how many.

Count the 👤 in each row.

Snack We Like					
🍎 apple	👤	👤	👤	👤	👤
🥨 pretzel	👤	👤	👤		

Each 👤 stands for I child who chose that snack.

There are __5__ children who chose 🍎.

There are __3__ children who chose 🥨.

Use the picture graph to answer each question.

What We Ate for Lunch							
🥪 sandwich	👤	👤	👤	👤	👤	👤	
🥫 soup	👤	👤					

Each 👤 stands for I child.

I. Which lunch did more children choose? Circle.

_____

2. How many children chose 🥪? _____ children

_____

3. How many children chose 🥫? _____ children

Read Picture Graphs

Our Favorite Outdoor Activity									
🚲 biking	🧍	🧍	🧍	🧍	🧍	🧍	🧍	🧍
🛹 skating	🧍	🧍						
🏃 running	🧍	🧍	🧍	🧍				

Each 🧍 stands for 1 child.

Use the picture graph to answer the question.

1. How many children chose 🚲?

   ____ children

2. How many children chose 🛹 and 🏃 altogether?

   ____ children

3. Which activity did the most children choose? Circle.

PROBLEM SOLVING REAL WORLD

Write a number sentence to solve the problem.
Use the picture graph at the top of the page.

4. How many more children chose 🚲 than 🏃?

   ____ more children

   ___ ◯ ___ ◯ ___

Make Picture Graphs

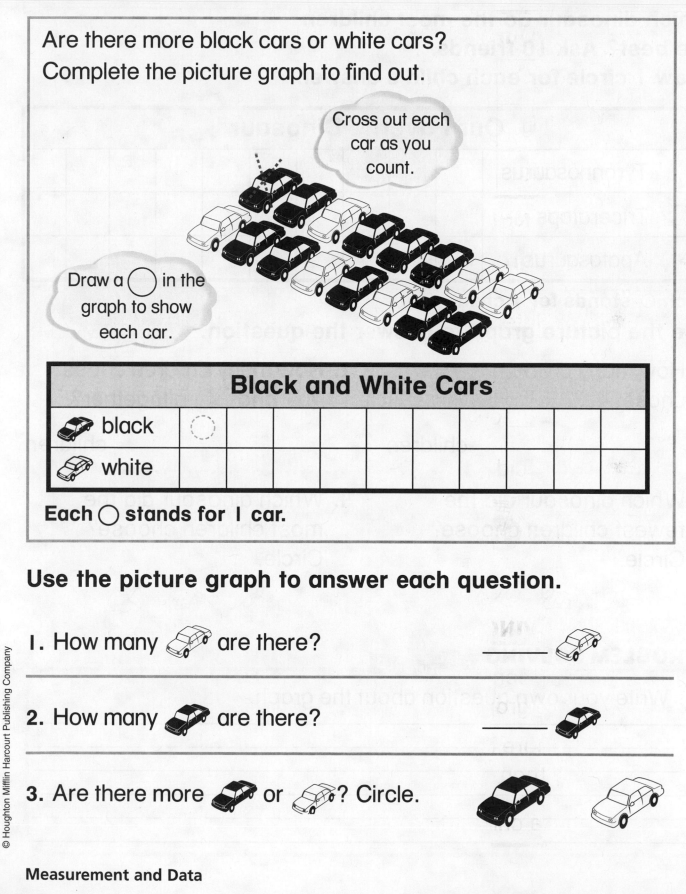

Are there more black cars or white cars?
Complete the picture graph to find out.

Cross out each car as you count.

Draw a ◯ in the graph to show each car.

Black and White Cars

	black										
🚗 black											
🚗 white											

Each ◯ stands for 1 car.

Use the picture graph to answer each question.

1. How many 🚗 are there? _____ 🚗

2. How many 🚗 are there? _____ 🚗

3. Are there more 🚗 or 🚗? Circle. 🚗 🚗

Make Picture Graphs

Which dinosaur do the most children
like best? Ask 10 friends.
Draw 1 circle for each child's answer.

Our Favorite Dinosaur										
🦖 Tyrannosaurus										
🦕 Triceratops										
🦕 Apatosaurus										

Each ○ stands for 1 child.

Use the picture graph to answer the question.

1. How many children
   chose 🦖 ?

   ____ children

2. How many children chose
   🦕 and 🦕 altogether?

   ____ children

3. Which dinosaur did the
   fewest children choose?
   Circle.

   🦖   🦕   🦕

4. Which dinosaur did the
   most children choose?
   Circle.

   🦖   🦕   🦕

PROBLEM SOLVING REAL WORLD

5. Write your own question about the graph.

   _____

   _____

   _____

   _____

Name _____

Lesson 81
COMMON CORE STANDARD CC.1.MD.4
Lesson Objective: Analyze and compare data shown in a bar graph.

Read Bar Graphs

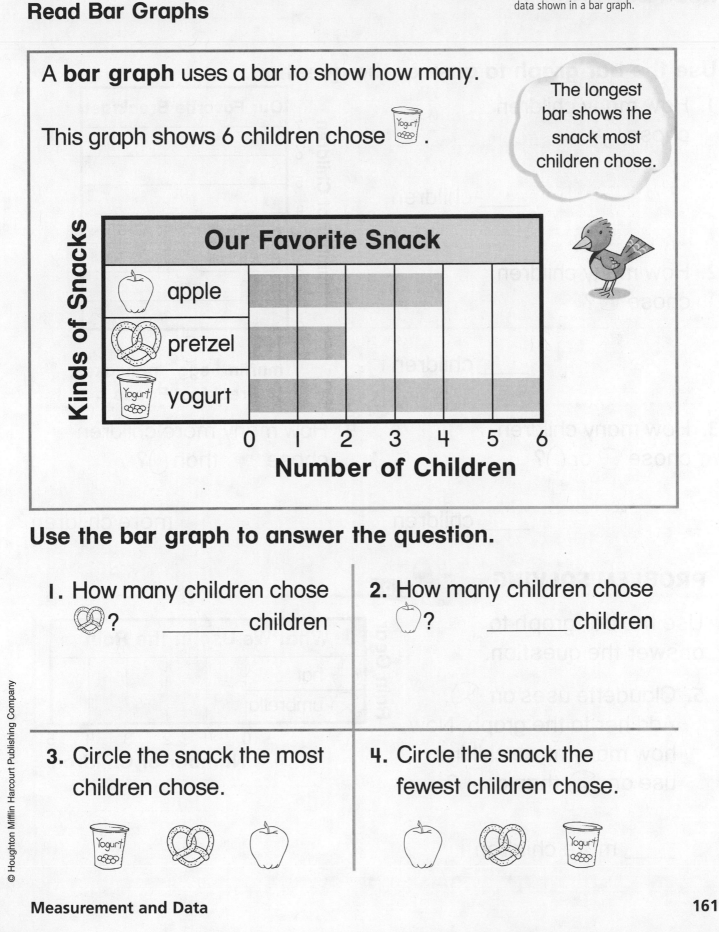

A **bar graph** uses a bar to show how many.

This graph shows 6 children chose .

The longest bar shows the snack most children chose.

Our Favorite Snack

Kinds of Snacks: apple, pretzel, yogurt

Number of Children: 0 1 2 3 4 5 6

Use the bar graph to answer the question.

1. How many children chose ⬭? _____ children

2. How many children chose 🍎? _____ children

3. Circle the snack the most children chose.

4. Circle the snack the fewest children chose.

Read Bar Graphs

Use the bar graph to answer the question.

1. How many children chose ◯?

   ____ children

2. How many children chose 🧁?

   ____ children

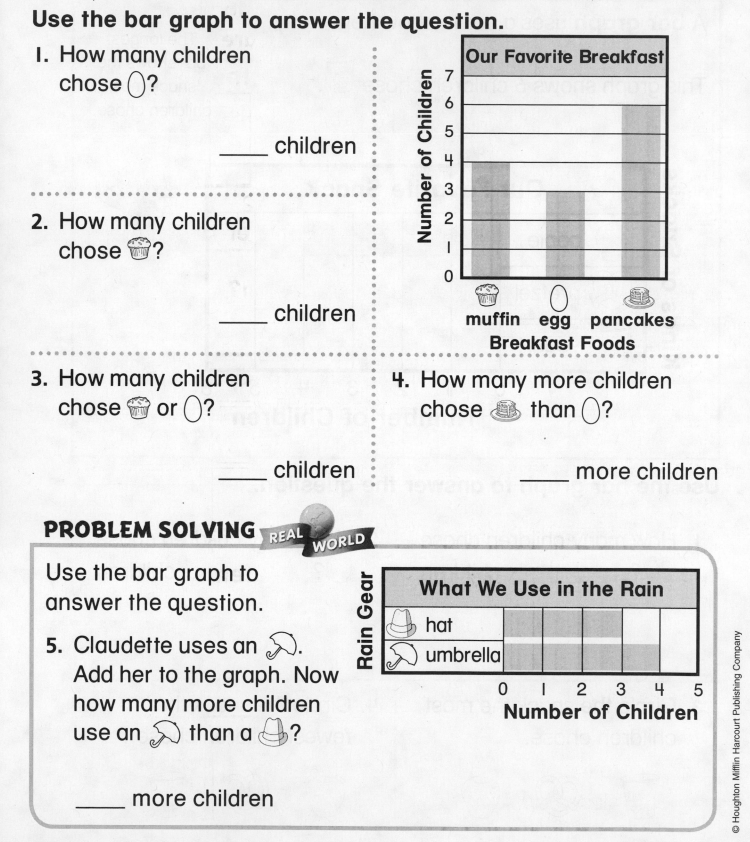

Our Favorite Breakfast

Number of Children

Breakfast Foods: muffin, egg, pancakes

3. How many children chose 🧁 or ◯?

   ____ children

4. How many more children chose 🥞 than ◯?

   ____ more children

PROBLEM SOLVING REAL WORLD

Use the bar graph to answer the question.

5. Claudette uses an ☂. Add her to the graph. Now how many more children use an ☂ than a 👒?

   ____ more children

What We Use in the Rain

Rain Gear: hat, umbrella

Number of Children 0 1 2 3 4 5

Lesson 82

COMMON CORE STANDARD CC.1.MD.4
Lesson Objective: Make a bar graph and interpret the information.

Make Bar Graphs

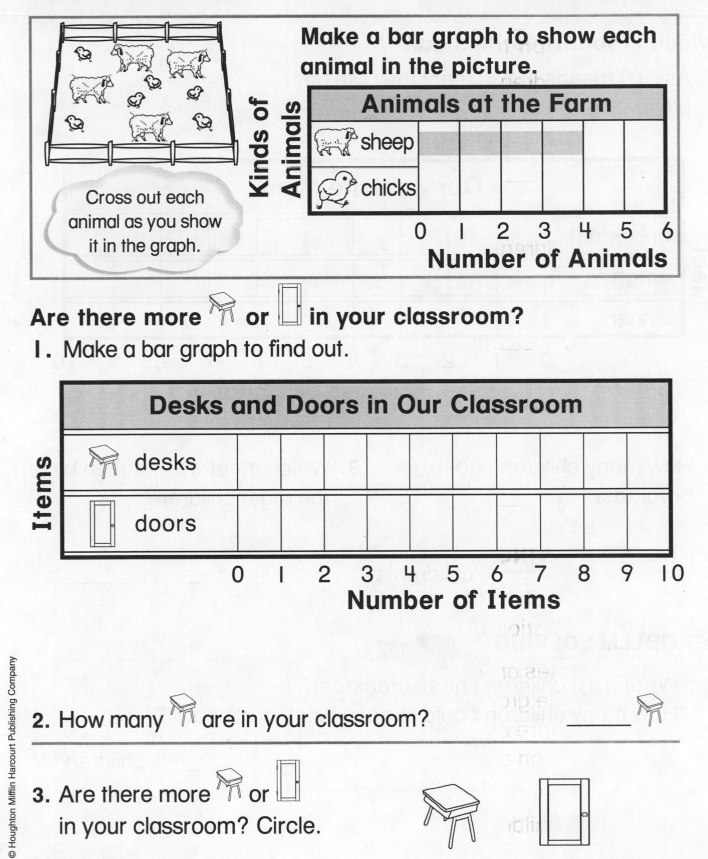

Make a bar graph to show each animal in the picture.

Cross out each animal as you show it in the graph.

Kinds of Animals

Animals at the Farm

| | sheep | | | | | | |
| | chicks | | | | | | |

0 1 2 3 4 5 6

Number of Animals

Are there more 🪑 or 🚪 in your classroom?

1. Make a bar graph to find out.

Items

Desks and Doors in Our Classroom

| | desks | | | | | | | | | |
| | doors | | | | | | | | | |

0 1 2 3 4 5 6 7 8 9 10

Number of Items

2. How many 🪑 are in your classroom? _____

3. Are there more 🪑 or 🚪 in your classroom? Circle.

Measurement and Data

Make Bar Graphs

Which is your favorite meal?

1. Ask 10 friends which meal they like best.
Make a bar graph.

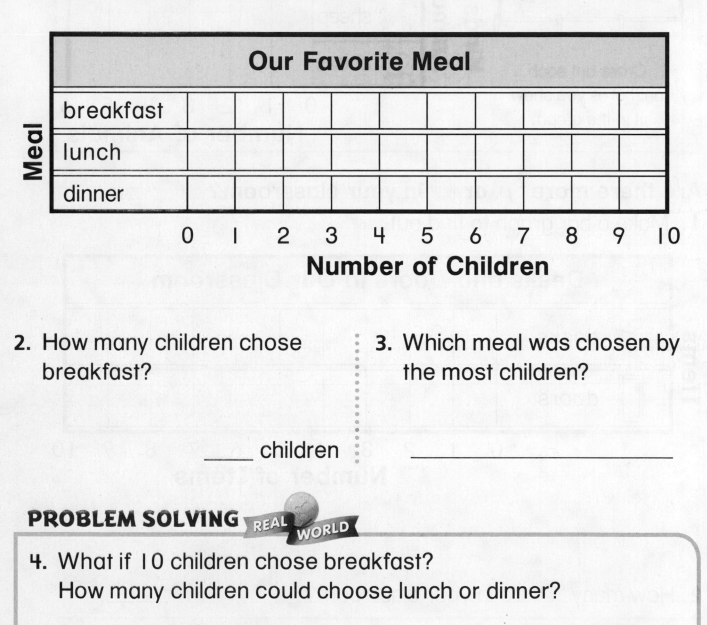

Our Favorite Meal

Meal										
breakfast										
lunch										
dinner										

0 1 2 3 4 5 6 7 8 9 10
Number of Children

2. How many children chose
breakfast?

_____ children

3. Which meal was chosen by
the most children?

_____

PROBLEM SOLVING REAL WORLD

4. What if 10 children chose breakfast?
How many children could choose lunch or dinner?

_____ children

Read Tally Charts

Some children named their favorite collections.

Each | stands for 1 child.

Each ||||| stands for 5 children.

Our Favorite Thing to Collect		Total
shells	|||| 1 2 3 4	4
stamps	|||| || 5 6 7	7

More children like to collect _____stamps_____.

Complete the tally chart.

Do you have a pet?		Total
yes	|||| |||	
no	||||	

Use the tally chart to answer each question.

1. How many children have a pet? _____ children

_____

2. How many children do not have a pet? _____ children

_____

3. Did more children answer yes or no? _____

_____

Measurement and Data

Read Tally Charts

Complete the tally chart.

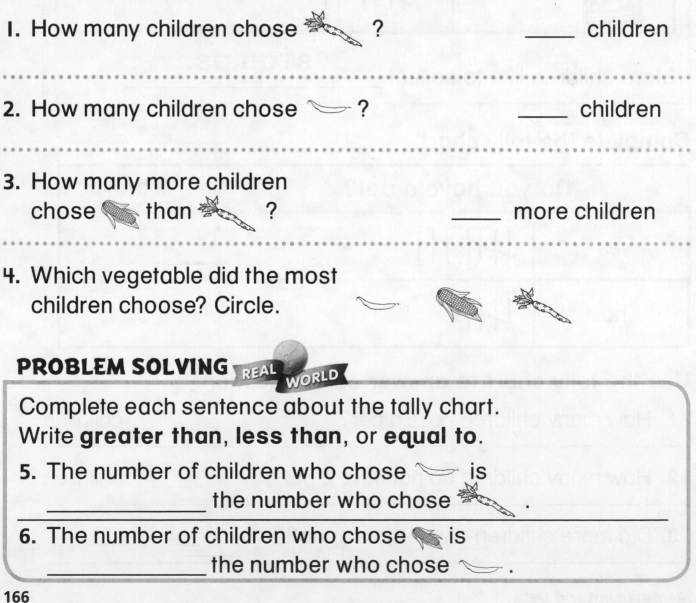

Our Favorite Vegetable		Total
beans	IIII	
corn	IIII III	
carrots	IIII	

Use the tally chart to answer each question.

1. How many children chose carrots?   _____ children

2. How many children chose beans?   _____ children

3. How many more children chose corn than carrots?   _____ more children

4. Which vegetable did the most children choose? Circle.

PROBLEM SOLVING REAL WORLD

Complete each sentence about the tally chart.
Write **greater than**, **less than**, or **equal to**.

5. The number of children who chose beans is
_____ the number who chose carrots.

6. The number of children who chose corn is
_____ the number who chose beans.

Name _____

Lesson 84

COMMON CORE STANDARD CC.1.MD.4

Lesson Objective: Make a tally chart and interpret the information.

Make Tally Charts

The picture shows shapes. Make a tally chart to show how many of each shape.

Cross out each shape as you count.

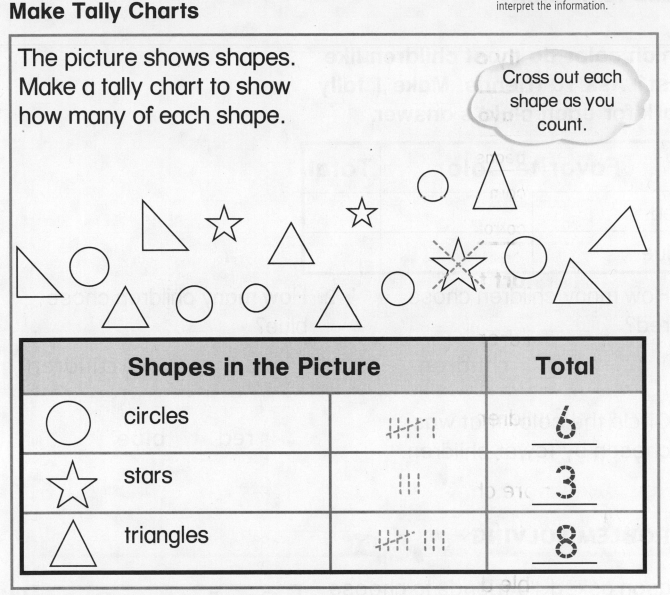

Shapes in the Picture		Total
⭕ circles	ⅢⅠⅠ	6
⭐ stars	Ⅲ	3
△ triangles	Ⅲ Ⅲ ⅠⅠⅠ	8

Use the tally chart to answer each question.

1. How many ☆ are there?

_____ ☆

2. How many more △ than ◯ are there?

_____ more △

3. Which shape is there the most of? Circle.

◯   ☆   △

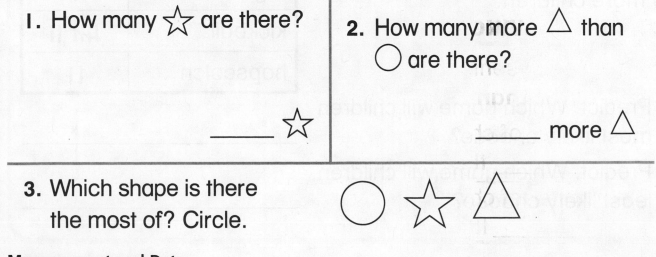

Make Tally Charts

Which color do most children like best? Ask 10 friends. Make 1 tally mark for each child's answer.

Favorite Color		Total
red		
blue		

1. How many children chose red?

_____ children

2. How many children chose blue?

_____ children

3. Circle the color that was chosen by fewer children.

red   blue

PROBLEM SOLVING REAL WORLD

Jason asked 10 friends to choose their favorite game. He will ask 10 more children.

Our Favorite Game	
tag	I
kickball	⊮⊮ II
hopscotch	II

4. Predict. Which game will children most likely choose?

_____

5. Predict. Which game will children least likely choose?

_____

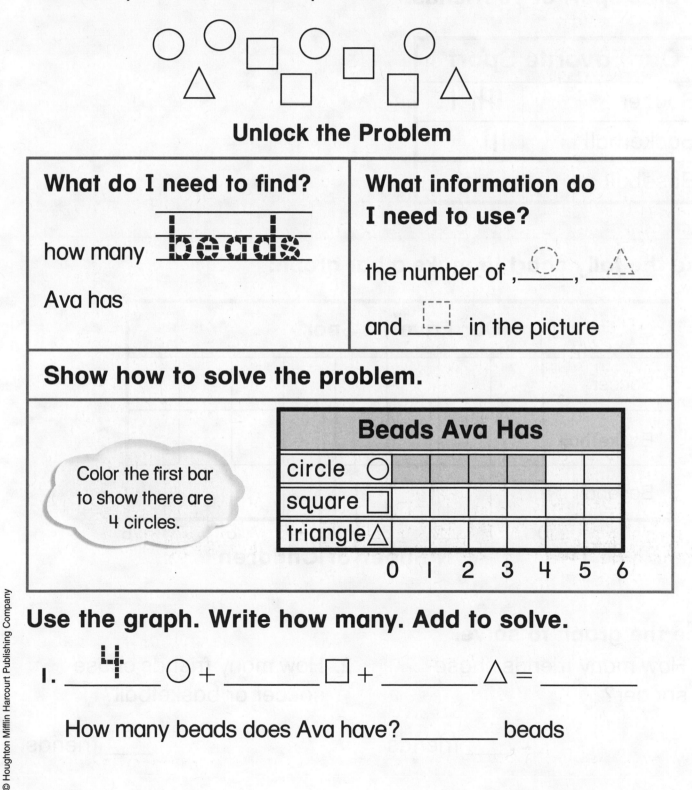

Name _____

Lesson 85

COMMON CORE STANDARD CC.1.MD.4

Lesson Objective: Solve problem situations using the strategy *make a graph*.

Problem Solving • Represent Data

Ava has these beads to make a bracelet.
How can you find how many beads she has?

Unlock the Problem

What do I need to find?	**What information do I need to use?**
how many **beads** Ava has	the number of , ____○ , ____△ and ____□ in the picture

Show how to solve the problem.

Color the first bar to show there are 4 circles.

Beads Ava Has

circle ○							
square □							
triangle △							

0　1　2　3　4　5　6

Use the graph. Write how many. Add to solve.

1. ___4___ ○ + _____ □ + _____ △ = _____

How many beads does Ava have? _____ beads

Problem Solving • Represent Data

Bella made a tally chart to show the
favorite sport of 10 friends.

Our Favorite Sport	
Soccer	‖‖ Ⅰ
Basketball	‖‖
Baseball	Ⅰ

Use the tally chart to make a bar graph.

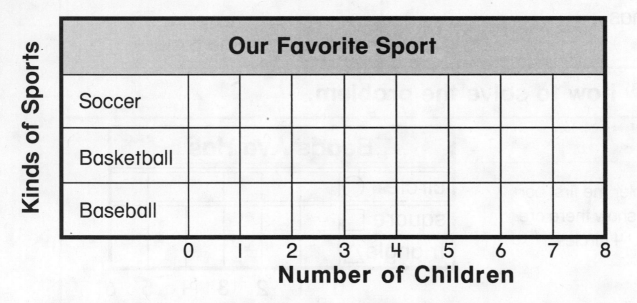

Use the graph to solve.

1. How many friends chose
   soccer?

   _____ friends

2. How many friends chose
   soccer or basketball?

   _____ friends

Three-Dimensional Shapes

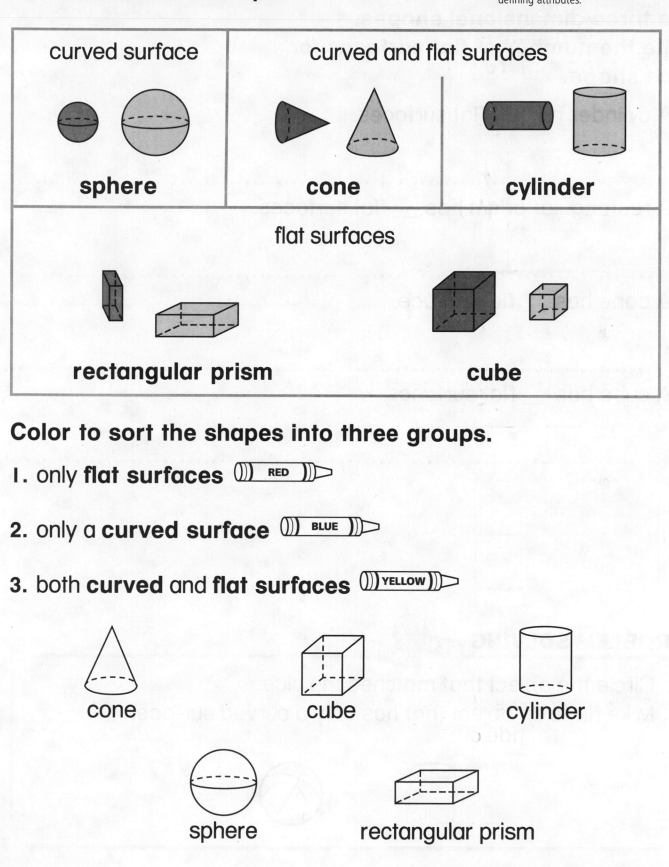

curved surface

sphere

curved and flat surfaces

cone

cylinder

flat surfaces

rectangular prism

cube

Color to sort the shapes into three groups.

1. only **flat surfaces** RED

2. only a **curved surface** BLUE

3. both **curved** and **flat surfaces** YELLOW

cone   cube   cylinder

sphere   rectangular prism

Three-Dimensional Shapes

Use three-dimensional shapes.
Write the number of flat surfaces for
each shape.

1. A cylinder has ___ flat surfaces.

....

2. A rectangular prism has ___ flat surfaces.

....

3. A cone has ___ flat surface.

....

4. A cube has ___ flat surfaces.

....

PROBLEM SOLVING REAL WORLD

5. Circle the object that matches the clue.
Mike finds an object that has only a curved surface.

Lesson 87

COMMON CORE STANDARD CC.1.G.1
Lesson Objective: Identify two-dimensional shapes on three-dimensional shapes.

Two-Dimensional Shapes
on Three-Dimensional Shapes

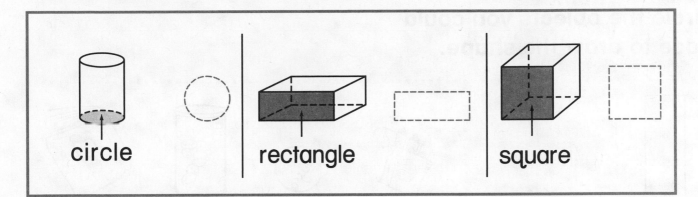

Look at the shape.
Circle the flat surfaces it has.

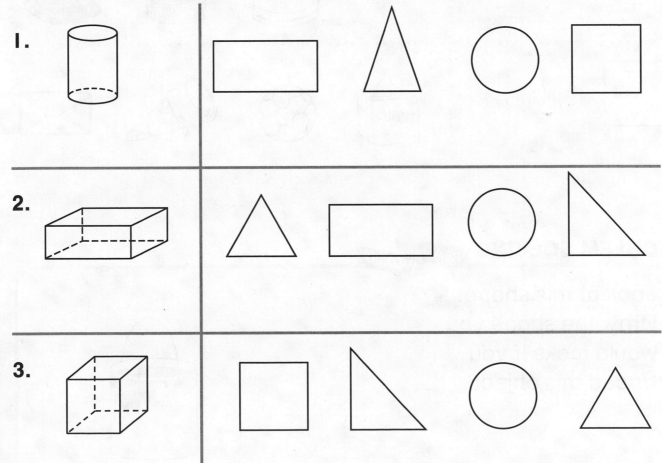

Name _____

Two-Dimensional Shapes on Three-Dimensional Shapes

Circle the objects you could trace to draw the shape.

1.

2.

3.

PROBLEM SOLVING REAL WORLD

4. Look at this shape. Draw the shape you would make if you traced this object.

Sort Two-Dimensional Shapes

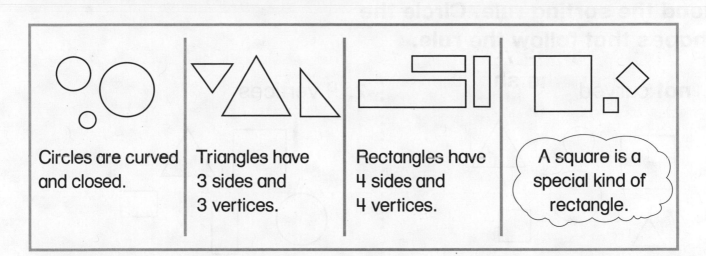

Circles are curved and closed.

Triangles have 3 sides and 3 vertices.

Rectangles have 4 sides and 4 vertices.

A square is a special kind of rectangle.

Read the sorting rule. Circle the shapes that follow the rule.

1. 4 sides

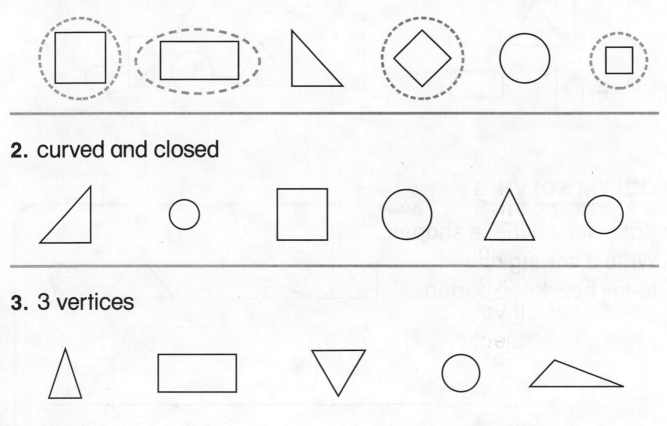

2. curved and closed

3. 3 vertices

Sort Two-Dimensional Shapes

**Read the sorting rule. Circle the
shapes that follow the rule.**

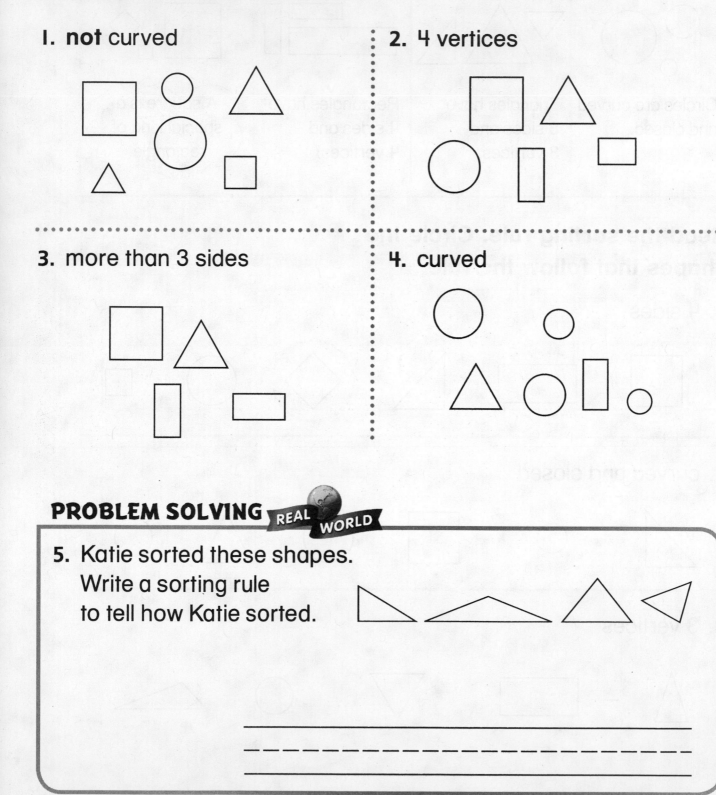

1. **not** curved

2. 4 vertices

3. more than 3 sides

4. curved

PROBLEM SOLVING REAL WORLD

5. Katie sorted these shapes.
Write a sorting rule
to tell how Katie sorted.

_____

_ _ _ _ _ _ _ _ _ _ _ _

_____

Lesson 89

COMMON CORE STANDARD CC.1.G.1
Lesson Objective: Describe attributes of two-dimensional shapes.

Describe Two-Dimensional Shapes

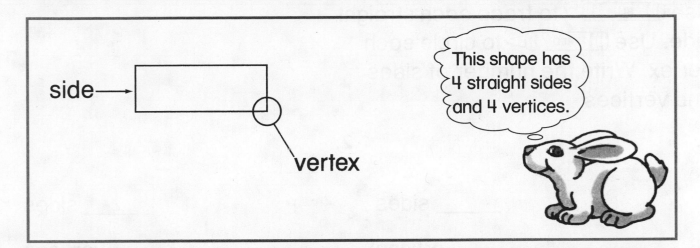

This shape has 4 straight sides and 4 vertices.

Write the number of straight sides or vertices.

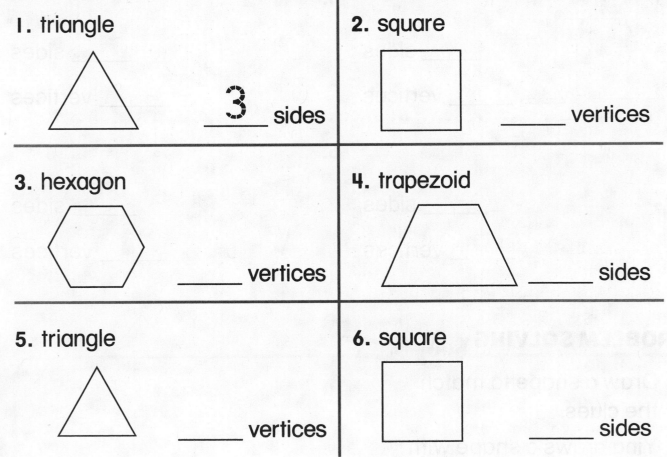

1. triangle

_____ **3** _____ sides

2. square

_____ vertices

3. hexagon

_____ vertices

4. trapezoid

_____ sides

5. triangle

_____ vertices

6. square

_____ sides

Name _____

Describe Two-Dimensional Shapes

Use 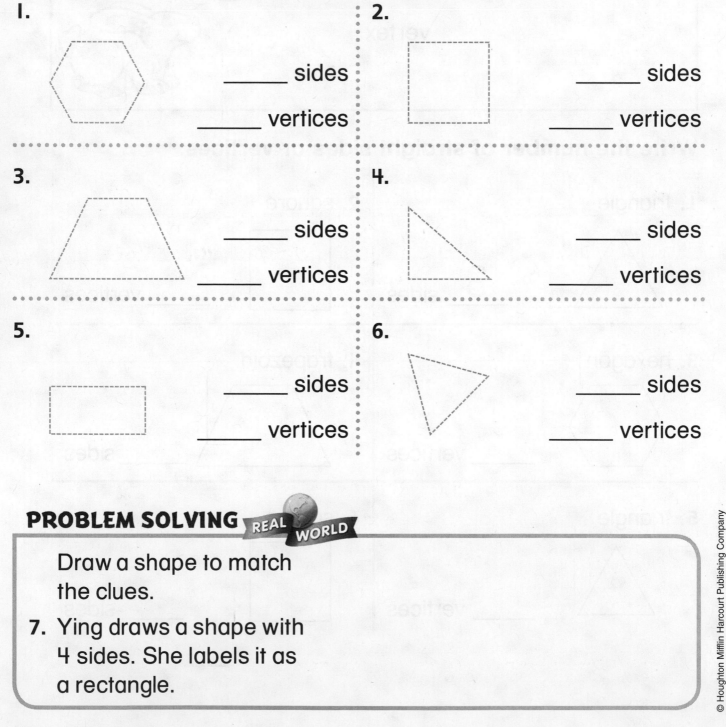 BLUE to trace each straight side. Use RED to circle each vertex. Write the number of sides and vertices.

1.

_____ sides

_____ vertices

2.

_____ sides

_____ vertices

3.

_____ sides

_____ vertices

4.

_____ sides

_____ vertices

5.

_____ sides

_____ vertices

6.

_____ sides

_____ vertices

PROBLEM SOLVING REAL WORLD

Draw a shape to match the clues.

7. Ying draws a shape with 4 sides. She labels it as a rectangle.

Combine Three-Dimensional Shapes

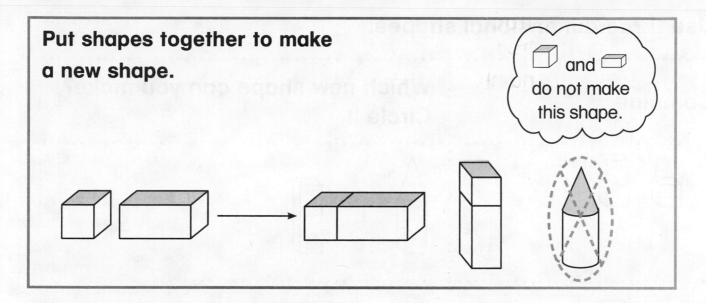

Put shapes together to make
a new shape.

and
do not make
this shape.

Use three-dimensional shapes.

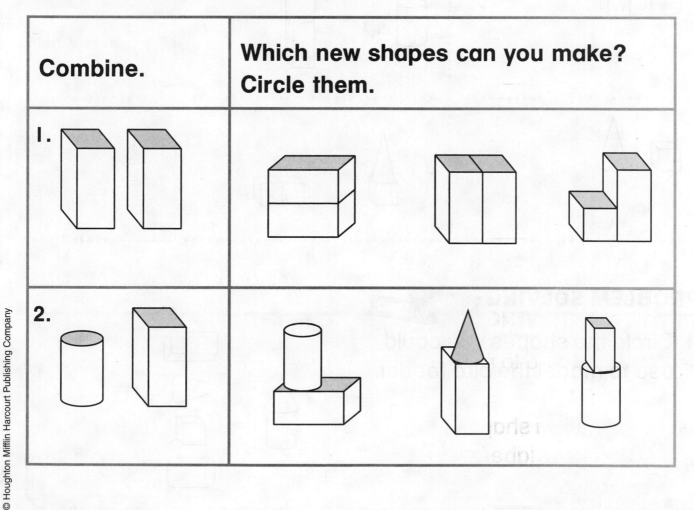

Combine.	Which new shapes can you make? Circle them.
1.	
2.	

Geometry

Combine Three-Dimensional Shapes

Use three-dimensional shapes.

Combine.

Which new shape can you make? Circle it.

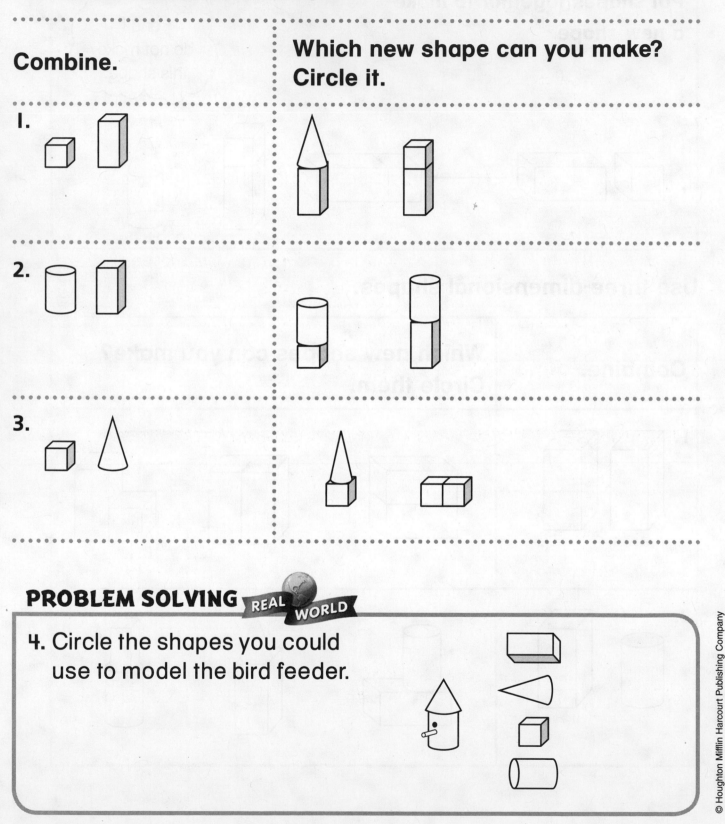

1.

2.

3.

© Houghton Mifflin Harcourt Publishing Company

PROBLEM SOLVING REAL WORLD

4. Circle the shapes you could use to model the bird feeder.

Lesson 91

COMMON CORE STANDARD CC.1.G.2
Lesson Objective: Use composite three-dimensional shapes to build new shapes.

Make New Three-Dimensional Shapes

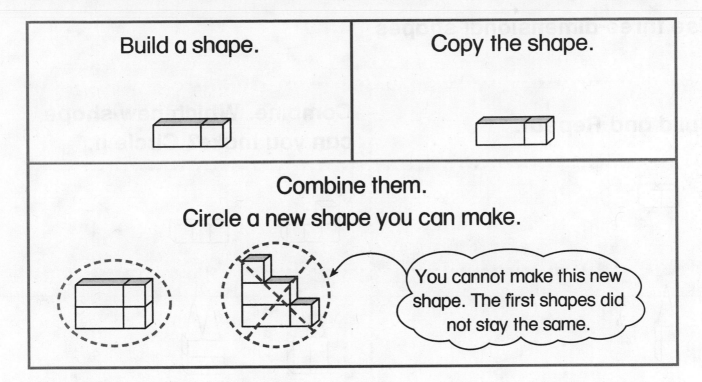

Build a shape.	Copy the shape.

Combine them.
Circle a new shape you can make.

You cannot make this new shape. The first shapes did not stay the same.

Use three-dimensional shapes.

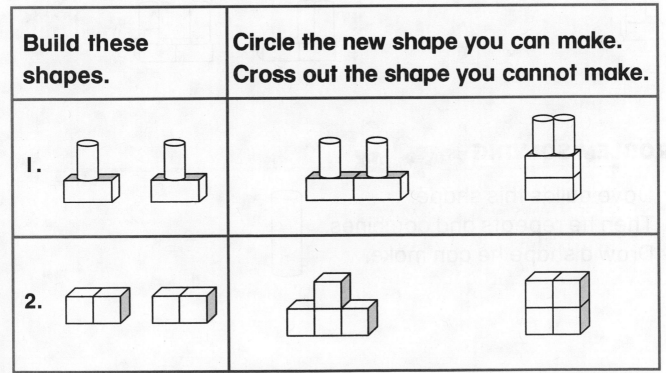

Build these shapes.	Circle the new shape you can make. Cross out the shape you cannot make.
1.	
2.	

Make New Three-Dimensional Shapes

Use three-dimensional shapes.

Build and Repeat.	**Combine. Which new shape can you make? Circle it.**

I.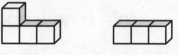

2.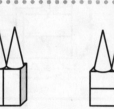

3.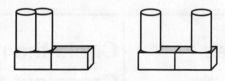

PROBLEM SOLVING REAL WORLD

4. Dave builds this shape.
   Then he repeats and combines.
   Draw a shape he can make.

Name _____

Lesson 92

COMMON CORE STANDARD CC.1.G.2

Lesson Objective: Identify three-dimensional shapes used to build a composite shape using the strategy *act it out*.

Problem Solving • Take Apart Three-Dimensional Shapes

Kate has △, ⬜, ◻, and ◻.
She built a tower.
Which shapes did Kate
use to build the tower?

Unlock the Problem

What do I need to find?	**What information do I need to use?**
which **shapes** Kate used to build the tower	Kate has these shapes. 

Show how to solve the problem. Find the matching shapes.

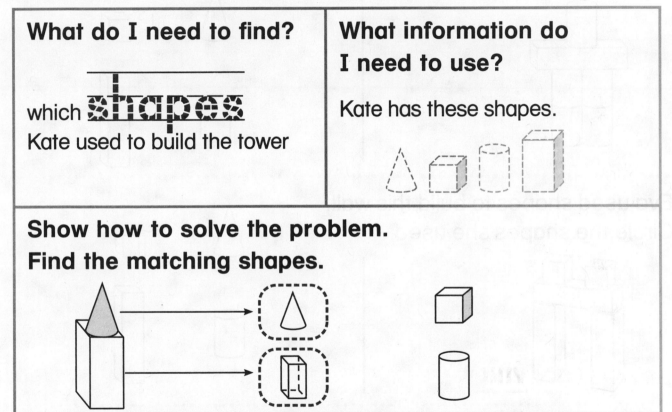

Use three-dimensional shapes. Circle your answer.

1. Which shapes did Marvin use to build this bench?

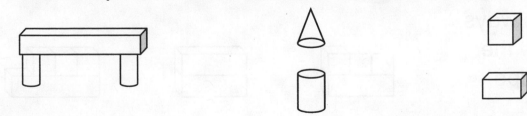

Problem Solving • Take Apart
Three-Dimensional Shapes

Use three-dimensional shapes.
Circle your answer.

1. Paco used shapes to build this robot. Circle the shapes he used.

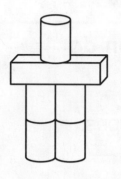

2. Eva used shapes to build this wall. Circle the shapes she used.

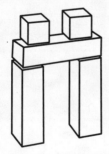

PROBLEM SOLVING REAL WORLD

3. Circle the ways that show the same shape.

Name _____

Lesson 93

COMMON CORE STANDARD CC.1.G.2

Lesson Objective: Use objects to compose new two-dimensional shapes.

Combine Two-Dimensional Shapes

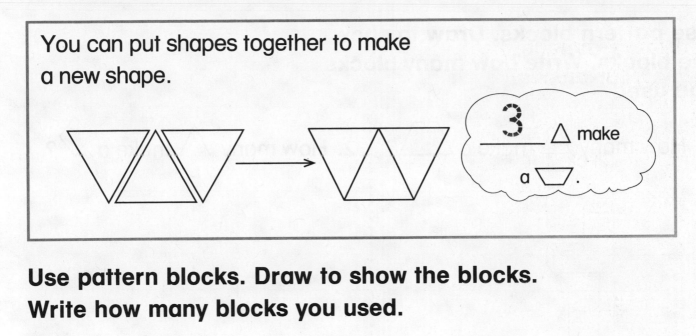

You can put shapes together to make a new shape.

___3___ △ make a ⏢.

Use pattern blocks. Draw to show the blocks.
Write how many blocks you used.

1. How many ⏢ make a ⬡?

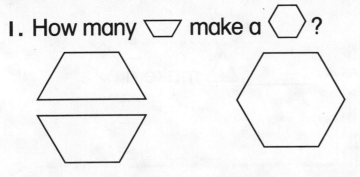

_____ ⏢ make a ⬡.

2. How many ◇ make a ⬡?

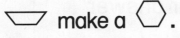

_____ ◇ make a ⬡.

Geometry

Combine Two-Dimensional Shapes

**Use pattern blocks. Draw to show
the blocks. Write how many blocks
you used.**

1. How many △ make a ⬜?

_____ △ make a ⬜.

2. How many △ make a ◇?

_____ △ make a ◇.

PROBLEM SOLVING REAL WORLD

Use pattern blocks. Draw to show your answer.

3. 2 ⬜ make a ⬡.

How many ⬜ make 4 ⬡?

_____ ⬜ make 4 ⬡.

Combine More Shapes

Combine shapes to make a new shape.

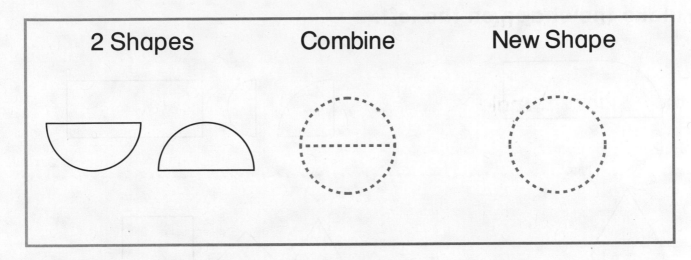

2 Shapes   Combine   New Shape

Circle the shapes that can combine to make the new shape.

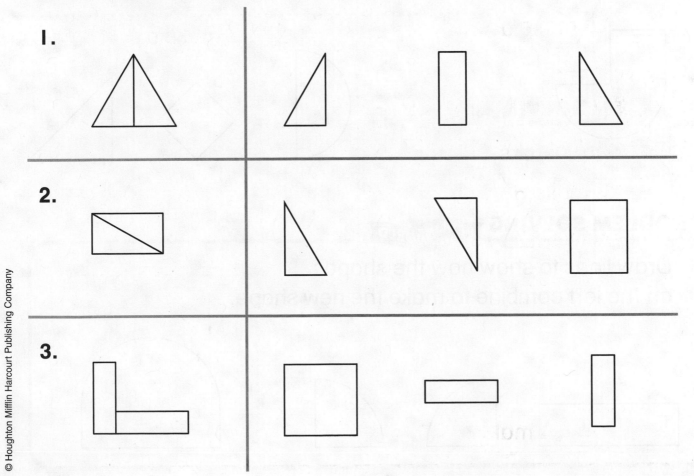

1.

2.

3.

Combine More Shapes

**Circle two shapes that can combine
to make the shape on the left.**

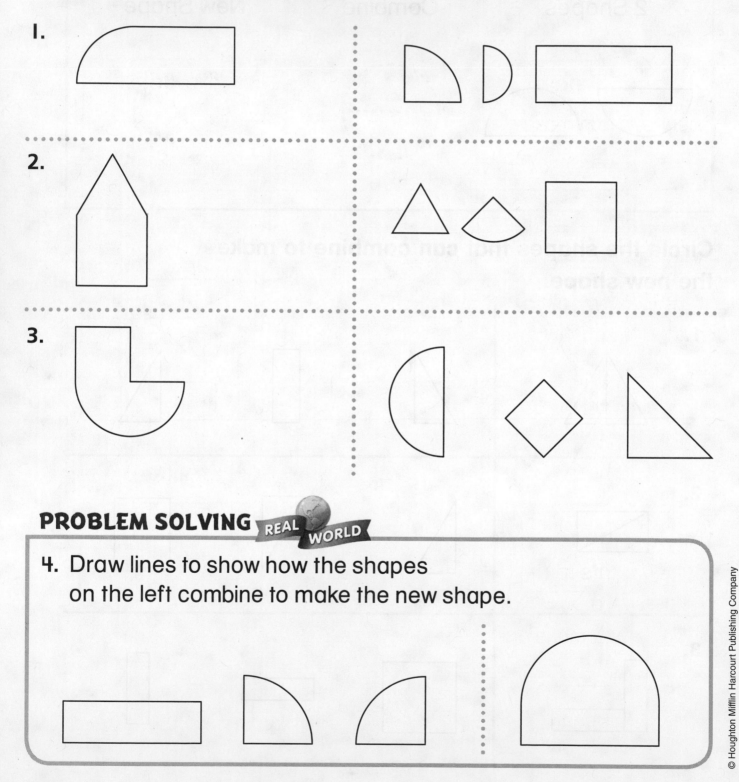

1.

2.

3.

PROBLEM SOLVING REAL WORLD

4. Draw lines to show how the shapes
   on the left combine to make the new shape.

Name _____

Lesson 95
COMMON CORE STANDARD CC.1.G.2
Lesson Objective: Make new shapes from composite two-dimensional shapes using the strategy *act it out*.

Problem Solving • Make New Two-Dimensional Shapes

Luis wants to use △ to make a ◇.
How many △ does he need?

Unlock the Problem

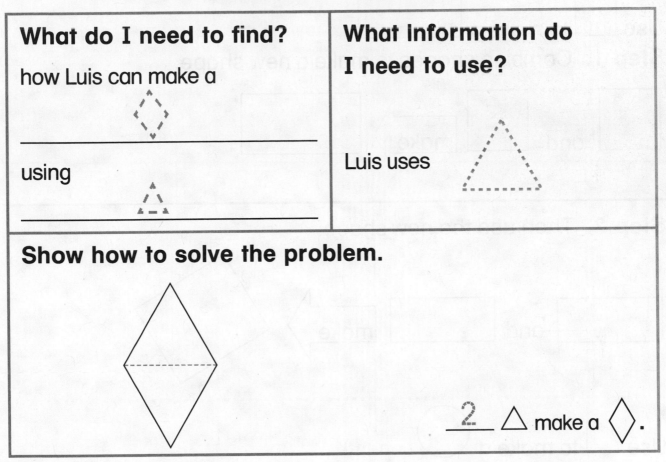

What do I need to find?

how Luis can make a

_____

using

_____

What information do I need to use?

Luis uses

Show how to solve the problem.

__2__ △ make a ◇.

Use shapes to solve.

1. Meg wants to use △
   to make a ▽ .
   _____ △ make a ▽ .

Problem Solving • Make New Two-Dimensional Shapes

Use shapes to solve.
Draw to show your work.

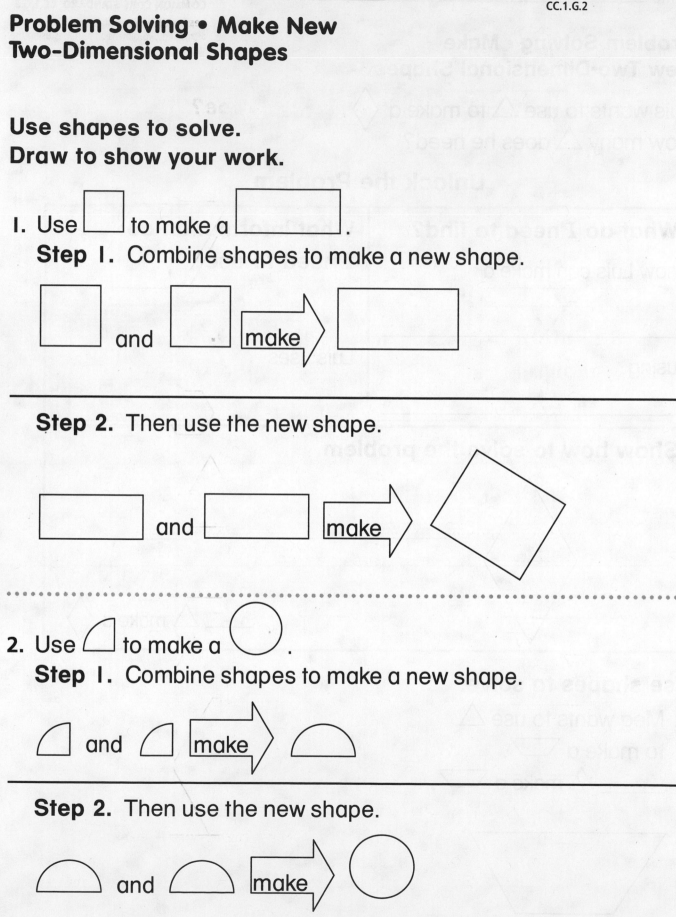

1. Use ☐ to make a ▭.

   Step 1. Combine shapes to make a new shape.

   ☐ and ☐ │make➜│ ▭

   Step 2. Then use the new shape.

   ▭ and ▭ │make➜│ ◇

2. Use ◿ to make a ◯.

   Step 1. Combine shapes to make a new shape.

   ◿ and ◿ │make➜│ ◠

   Step 2. Then use the new shape.

   ◠ and ◠ │make➜│ ◯

Find Shapes in Shapes

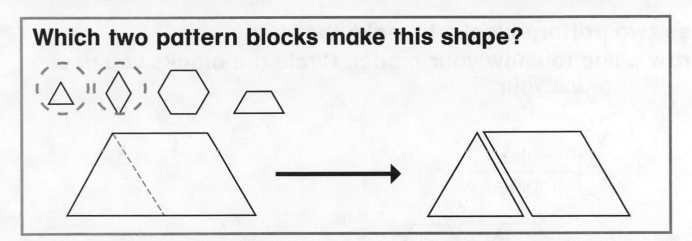

Which two pattern blocks make this shape?

Use two pattern blocks to make the shape.

Circle the blocks you use.

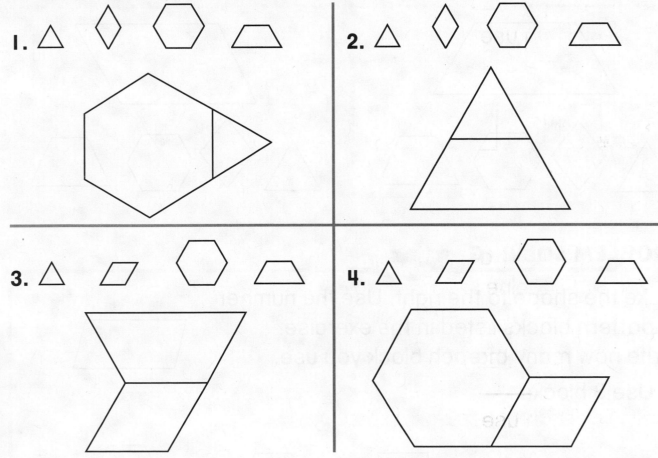

1.

2.

3.

4.

Find Shapes in Shapes

Use two pattern blocks to make the shape.
Draw a line to show your model. Circle the blocks you use.

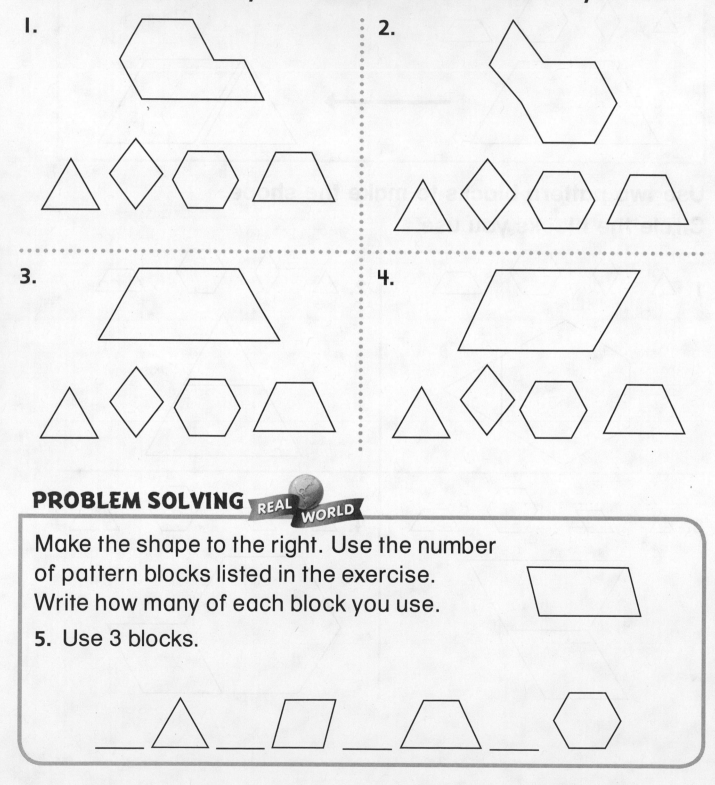

1.

2.

3.

4.

PROBLEM SOLVING REAL WORLD

Make the shape to the right. Use the number
of pattern blocks listed in the exercise.
Write how many of each block you use.

5. Use 3 blocks.

_____ _____ _____ _____

Name _____

Lesson 97
COMMON CORE STANDARD CC.1.G.2
Lesson Objective: Decompose two-dimensional shapes into parts.

Take Apart Two-Dimensional Shapes

Use pattern blocks to help you find the parts of a shape.

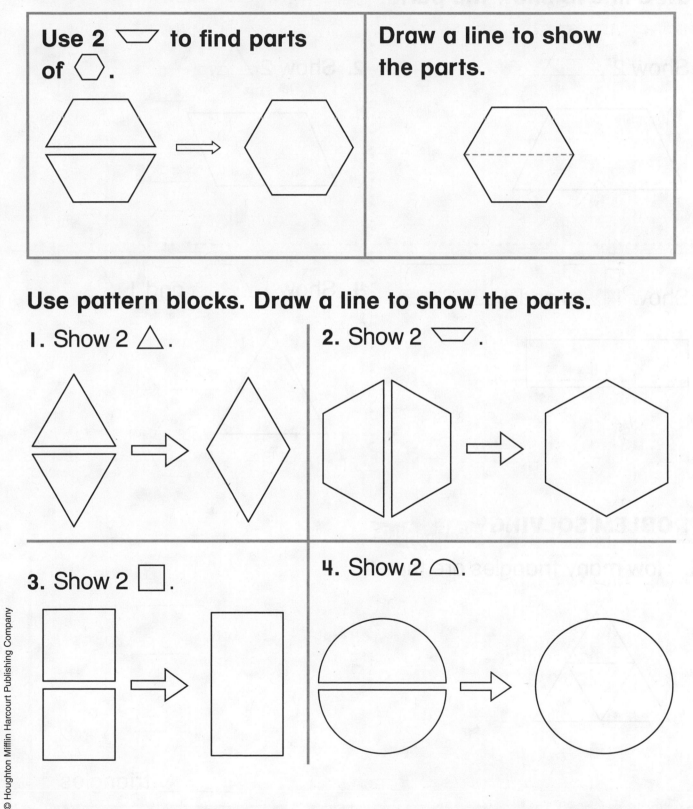

Use pattern blocks. Draw a line to show the parts.

1. Show 2 △.

2. Show 2 ▽.

3. Show 2 □.

4. Show 2 ◠.

Take Apart Two-Dimensional Shapes

Draw a line to show the parts.

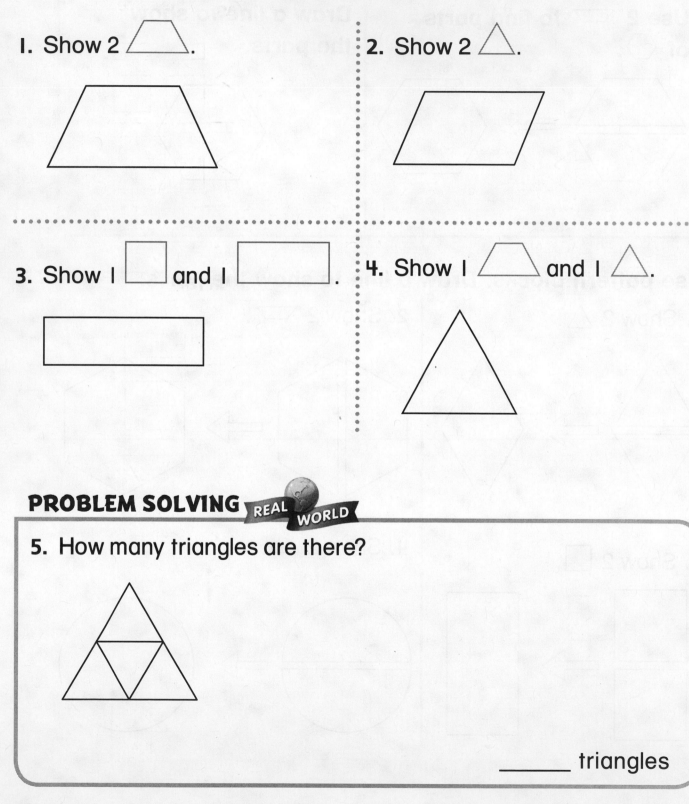

1. Show 2 ⬭.

2. Show 2 △.

3. Show 1 ☐ and 1 ▭.

4. Show 1 ⬭ and 1 △.

PROBLEM SOLVING REAL WORLD

5. How many triangles are there?

_____ triangles

Lesson 98

COMMON CORE STANDARD CC.1.G.3

Lesson Objective: Identify equal and unequal parts (or shares) in two-dimensional shapes.

Equal or Unequal Parts

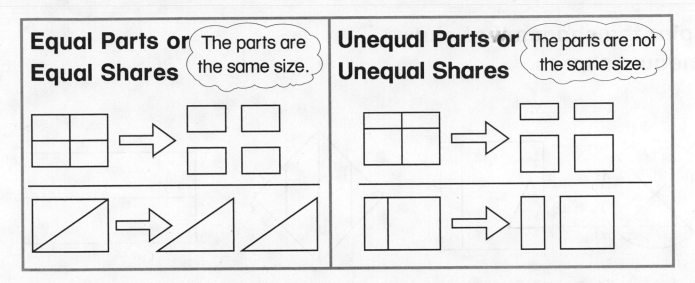

Equal Parts or Equal Shares — The parts are the same size.

Unequal Parts or Unequal Shares — The parts are not the same size.

Circle the shapes that show equal parts.
Cross out the shapes that show unequal parts.

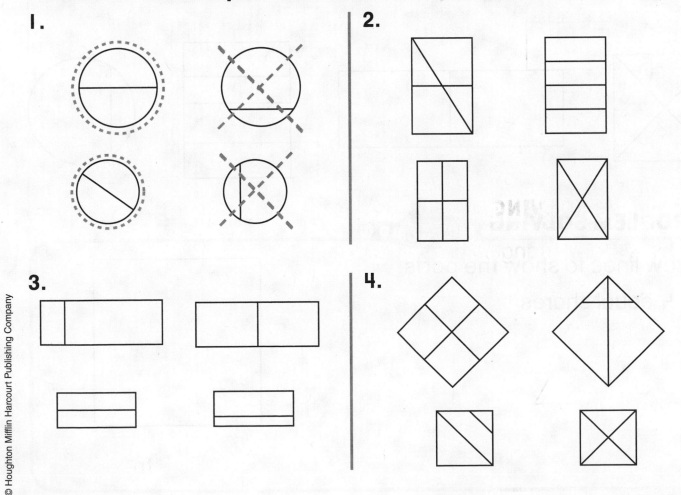

1.

2.

3.

4.

Name _____

Equal or Unequal Parts

**Color the shapes that show
unequal shares.**

1.

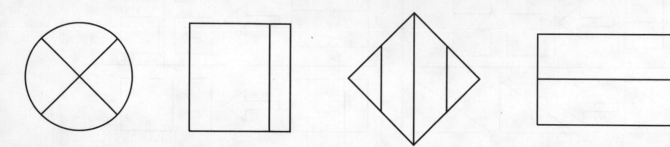

· ·

Color the shapes that show equal shares.

2.

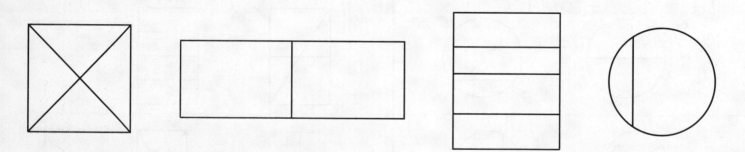

PROBLEM SOLVING REAL WORLD

Draw lines to show the parts.

3. 4 equal shares

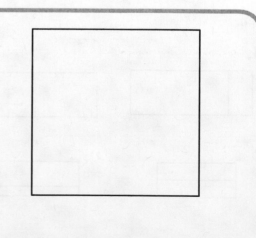

Halves

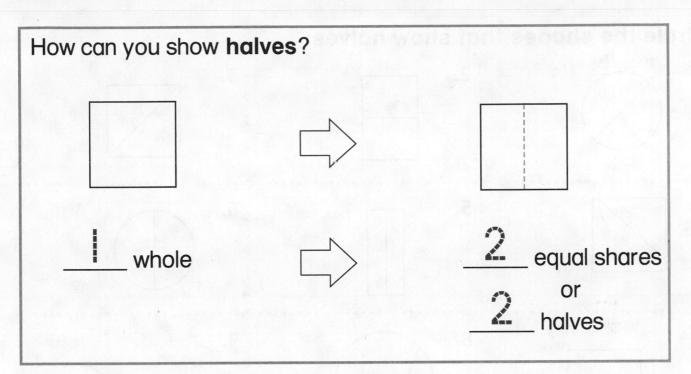

How can you show **halves**?

___|___ whole

___2___ equal shares
or
___2___ halves

Draw a line to show halves. Write the numbers.

1.

_____ whole   _____ halves

2.

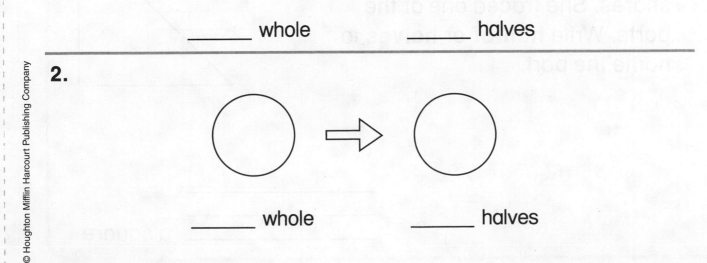

_____ whole   _____ halves

Halves

Circle the shapes that show halves.

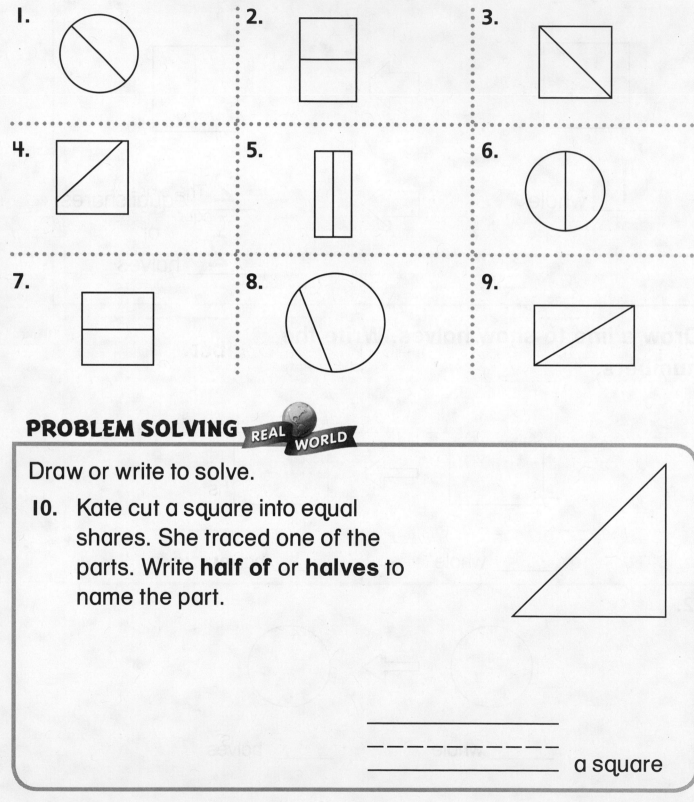

1.

2.

3.

4.

5.

6.

7.

8.

9.

PROBLEM SOLVING REAL WORLD

Draw or write to solve.

10. Kate cut a square into equal shares. She traced one of the parts. Write **half of** or **halves** to name the part.

_____

_ _ _ _ _ _ _ _ _ _

_____ a square

Name _____

Lesson 100

COMMON CORE STANDARD CC.1.G.3
Lesson Objective: Partition circles and rectangles into four equal shares.

Fourths

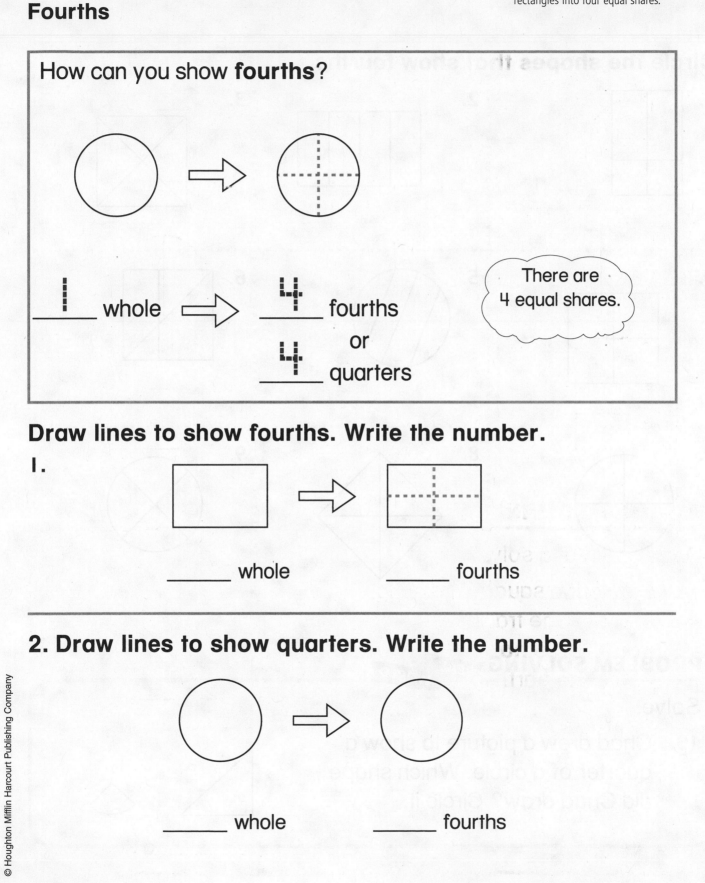

How can you show **fourths**?

_____ whole ⇒ _____ fourths
or
_____ quarters

There are 4 equal shares.

Draw lines to show fourths. Write the number.

1.

_____ whole   _____ fourths

2. Draw lines to show quarters. Write the number.

_____ whole   _____ fourths

Name _____

Fourths

Circle the shapes that show fourths.

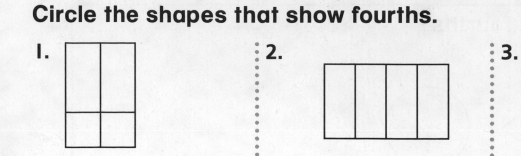

1.

2.

3.

4.

5.

6.

7.

8.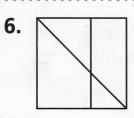

9.

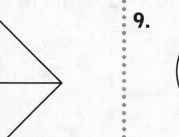 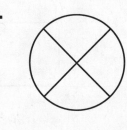

PROBLEM SOLVING REAL WORLD

Solve.

10. Chad drew a picture to show a quarter of a circle. Which shape did Chad draw? Circle it.

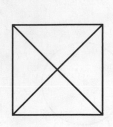